Dedicated to

*The daughters of the world who add sweetness
and light to our existence*

This WAY is EASIER, DAD

How my DAUGHTER SAVED ME from GROWING UP!

HARIMOHAN PARUVU

JAICO PUBLISHING HOUSE

Ahmedabad Bangalore Bhopal Bhubaneswar Chennai
Delhi Hyderabad Kolkata Lucknow Mumbai

Published by Jaico Publishing House
A-2 Jash Chambers, 7-A Sir Phirozshah Mehta Road
Fort, Mumbai - 400 001
jaicopub@jaicobooks.com
www.jaicobooks.com

© Harimohan Paruvu

THIS WAY IS EASIER DAD!
ISBN 978-93-86348-12-8

First Jaico Impression: 2017

No part of this book may be reproduced or utilized in
any form or by any means, electronic or
mechanical including photocopying, recording or by any
information storage and retrieval system,
without permission in writing from the publishers.

Page design and layout:
Geniies IT & Services Private Limited, Coimbatore

CONTENTS

HOW TO DEAL WITH THE WORLD	**1**
Making Peace With Ants That Bite	3
Birds Are Different From Humans, Right?	6
Enjoy the Wibbly-Wobbly Airplane Rides	8
Old Flowers For New Flowers	10
The Great Guitar Agitation	12
Heads I Win, Tails You Lose	15
Repaying Amaan's Kindness With Interest	17
I Have a Role to Play	19
So, You Call!	21
A Gift From ME to ME	23
Stop Cheating the Bees	25
We Didn't Discover The Zero	27
I Don't Care If Michael Jackson Is Black or White	29
Let Them Do Their Job, You Do Yours	31
Hand-written Letters and Land Line Phones	33
Be Good To Yourself First	35
Throw Those Candies, *Nanna!*	37
The Dog Protests	39
Give Up My Subsidy - Now	44
Plucking and Praying	46
An Interview with a Four-Year-Old	48

## How To Be Happy and How To Love and Be Loved	**53**

The Secret to a Happy World	54
To Get Loads of Love, Expect It Everywhere	56
There's Peace in War	58
To Get More Love, Love More People	61
The Magic Wand of Happiness	63
You Can Be Happy When You Win	65
And Remember… Everyone Loves You	68
Thanks for Digging the Road, Guys	70
We Can Build It Again	72
Can't Promise if I'll Love You in the Future	74
The Sentimental Saga of Rickety Lifts	76
Look At What You Are Getting!	78
We Are All Verbs	80
We Don't Need to Know Anything More – Go for It	82
Thanks for the Power (Cut) Guys	84
When We're Equal, We're Happy	86
The Putting-Smiles-On-Strangers-Faces Challenge	88
A Thoughtful Gift on Friendship-Day	91
Interview with a Four-and-a-Half-Year-Old	94

## How To Deal With People	**97**

My Team Has To Play	98
Welcome To Life At My Level	101
Give Only When Asked	103
Is Hugging Boys Bad?	105
Adding to the Green Day Pot	107
Good Teachers and Bad Teachers	110
We Don't Know if They Are Happy	112
My Friends Are Different Parts of Me	114
If You Can't Appreciate – Shut Up!	116
I Can Support Your Opponent For You	118
The Unforgettable Fruit Day Incident	121
A Surprise Gift For Harsh	124

Contents

A Lesson in Energy Management	127
A Master Class in Coaching	129
The Two Ways to Get Things Done	132
Could We Be More Polite Please?	134
They Copy Actions, Not Words	136
Interview with a Five-Year-Old	138

How To Approach Life — 143

It's Not the Size Dummy; It's the Learning	144
Learning Quickly Through Imitation	148
The Great Car Cleaning Project	150
The Knight Is Clever Only If We Are Clever	153
Try It First, And Then Decide	155
Why Feel What You Don't Feel	157
Let Us Go Only if It's Important	159
The Pineapple Juice is Not Good Or Bad	161
Computers versus Type Writers	163
But You're So Lucky	165
Can We Focus on What's Working	167
Ten Good Things Of The Day	169
Crime and Punishment	171
Spending Time With Myself	174
What Would I Like to Learn	176
Learning to Bicycle	178
I Can Learn By Myself –If You Give Me Your Phone	180
Interview With a Six-and-a-Half Year-Old	183

How To Get Things Done — 189

How To Play a Game Right	190
The Power of Three Boons	193
The Secret Formula for Success	196
Are Snakes Ladders Too	198
Lessons from a Soccer Game	201
We Play Fully When We Play a Match	204
Do Things You Don't Like First	206

Taking the High Performance Route at Golconda	208
A New Definition of a Loser	211
Add Challenge to Boring Jobs	213
The Happy Rakhi Day Startup	216
I'll Beat Yasvantt Someday	219
Organizing My Birthday Party	222
Performing Without Pressure	225
I'll Learn From My Mistakes the Hard Way	227
The 'Lucky Lemons' Lemonade Stall	229
Imagine There Is Nothing To Do, Then Pick One	233
Finish The Job First, Smile Later	235
Using Feedback to Learn Faster	237
Let's Go Jogging	239
Interview with a Seven-Year-Old	242

How To Flow With Abundance — 251

The Art of Receiving	252
A Lesson in Money Consciousness	254
Keep the Flow Going, Every Little Helps	257
Don't Think So Much - Buy It	259
A Child's Perspective About Money	261
Be In The Flow - Money Will Come, Money Will Go	264
You're Not The Buying Type	266
A Thoughtful Anniversary Gift	268

PART 1

HOW TO DEAL WITH THE WORLD

1
Making Peace With Ants That Bite

Anjali was playing in the backyard one tranquil afternoon when an ant bit her. The two-year-old was stunned. She did not expect the tiny ants to bite so ferociously for no reason. The pain and crying subsided in a day. But the fear remained.

Two days after the great betrayal, Anjali and I set out to the neighbourhood park. Our sedate five-minute walk turned into a dramatic 20-minute voyage. Anjali saw ants everywhere – black ants, red ants – many potential attackers crawling around ominously. The world, she discovered, was full of ants. She pointed at them as if asking – what do I do with them *Nanna*?

I revealed some of the ant secrets that I had learned in my day. I explained that red ants have a mean bite, small black ants are harmless and big black ants stay away if left alone. She listened carefully and repeated after me, holding on to this lifeline. The ants would not go away. She had to deal with them. Somehow.

Back at home that day, a lone black ant approached her. She checked with me. "Small black ants don't bite *na*." I nodded. Anjali held her ground. The ant looked at her and then went on its way. Anjali looked at me, relieved.

Life must be difficult for the two-year-old. But she finds ways to coexist.

A couple of weeks after the ant-bite episode, Anjali spotted a group of red ants (Danger No. 1 in my list) in the backyard. "Will the red ants bite?" She asked pointing them out to me. I told her they certainly would and advised her to stay far away from the mean little fellows if she did not want to get bitten again. She told me that they were carrying grains of rice. I said that they were perhaps storing food to eat, and went back to work.

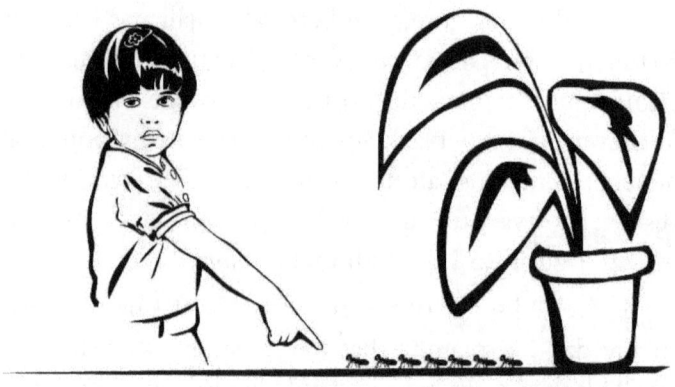

After a while Shobha called me to witness an unusual gathering in the backyard. Anjali had decided that the ants have nothing to eat for all their hard work. She gave them some sugar. The fierce red ants responded with gusto and crowded around the feast that Anjali literally threw for them.

I asked Anjali why she gave sugar to the ants. "Because they don't have anything to eat," she said and ran away. All the hurt and fear from the earlier incident had vanished. All that mattered now was that they had nothing to eat.

My way of handling past hurt is to hold on to the hurt, reject all concerned parties, make the issue bigger and make life miserable for myself. Then, wonder why I feel alone and hurt. Can I make life easier by releasing past hurt and moving on? Maybe give some sugar even?

A Return Gift for You: You flow easily when you do not reject people, situations and ideas because of one bad experience. You can access all possibilities if you can find ways to coexist. Holding on to past grudges weighs you down. Let go and flow.

Birds Are Different From Humans, Right?

Anjali and I were walking in the park. We saw some birds.

I wondered aloud how different the lives of birds were from ours.

"They build nests by themselves, search for food everyday and sleep in the open rain, or shine," I told her. "No school, no television, no brushing teeth, no doctor. Imagine living like that."

Anjali heard me out patiently.

"But we are all so different *Nanna*," she said after some thought. "Birds will do their things, animals will do their things and we will do our things. Even you and I are different because we do different things no. That's all. Everyone will do what they can."

I agree. There's no point trying to club and categorize. Let each one be.

I went back to watching the birds. This time, quietly.

My way of appreciating diversity is to present the others in a manner that makes me superior to them, gently show the others in bad light and make it all about me in the end. Then, wonder why the world thinks I am not really sensitive to diversity. Can I stop feeling superior? Or inferior?

A Return Gift for You: To be at peace and retain a sense of wonder, accept people and things the way they are. You open up possibilities when you do not generalize, separate and reject. Let each one be.

Enjoy the Wibbly-Wobbly Airplane Rides

We were flying home from Bangalore to Hyderabad by Air India. It's my favourite airline, mainly for its non-intrusive ways. The planes are bigger and appear to be stabler. The hostesses seem to know what to do in case of an emergency. And there is always something to eat. All in all – it is solid and dependable.

But this was an old flight and had its fair share of problems. The reading light would not work, the switch hung lifelessly, the button that gets the seat to recline was stuck leaving me seated at an odd angle and worst of all, the food was not too great. I was busy judging and feeling let down.

Anjali had a window seat. She was in good spirits. She would be – she was not piling up a list of judgments and opinions like me. She gazed out of the window and enjoyed the ride.

The aircraft hit bad weather. We suddenly dropped altitude. My ears ached. The plane rocked this way and that, lurching wildly. Seasoned travelers clutched seat handles, closed their eyes and started praying. It was quite bad.

We were tense with all the rocking and rolling. Then we heard a chirpy voice. "It's okay if it (the ride) is not smooth *Mamma*," said an obviously delighted Anjali. "I am enjoying myself in this wibbly-wobbly airplane."

Wibbly-wobbly airplane? She made it sound like she was on a toy ride in a park.

The irony struck me then. While we were looking at the worst possible outcome, Anjali was looking at the best outcome in the situation. A wibbly-wobbly airplane is as much fun as a ride in an entertainment park and not necessarily a death trap. We achieved nothing by worrying anyway.

My way of dealing with sudden, unforeseen change in my life is to imagine the worst possible outcomes, make doomsday predictions and scare myself to death. Then, wonder why life is such a scary experience. Can I see a beautiful outcome in every experience?

A Return Gift for You: While dealing with stressful situations, reframe the context and see the best possible outcomes, the fun and exciting possibilities in it. When you can see the best outcomes in the situation, you could well influence the result. Reframe and hold.

4
Old Flowers For New Flowers

I plucked a new rose, fresh from the garden to replace a bunch of withered three-day old flowers in the vase.

I gave Anjali the new rose. I expected her to throw away the old ones and keep the fresh one. But apparently she had other ideas. After a while she called out to me. "See," she said, pointing to the vase. The fresh red rose had now joined the dying flowers in the vase.

"So she won't feel lonely," she said. "Now they can all be together as friends."

Yes, of course. The young and the beautiful could feel lonely and frightened too. I never thought of that. They could be friends with the old and the dying. Maybe, instead of the old diminishing the beauty of the new, the new one may enhance the beauty of the old ones. Maybe they would even add a mature perspective to the new rose. One need not be at the cost of the other; everyone has a role to play.

My way of dealing with differences is to choose one end of the spectrum and reject the other when there is no need to choose between them, thus missing a million possibilities in between. Then, wonder why life is so boring. Can I be more aware of the prejudices that I carry?

 A Return Gift for You: To enjoy the beauty and harmony of life, include all, and exclude none. Everything has a place.

5. The Great Guitar Agitation

For the first time in her four years, Anjali used an organized protest against us. Miffed with the establishment that did not concede to her demand of a toy guitar (and instead gave her a downscale doll), she used her new found weapon – education - to protest.

Anjali had learned to write 'No' and 'Yes' and the two words were all she needed to launch her agitation. So she drew a guitar and wrote a large 'NO' on a Post-It and stuck it on my desk. The sign glowered at the management (me!) everyday from the desktop, reminding me of the demands of the four-year-old, the silent protest of the deprived. Her ominous protest, her non-violent agitation, was limited to this small note and the sad faces that she made at the management now and then. I waited for her next move.

The Agitation Intensifies

The agitation quickly spread to public areas. The main entrance of the house carried the now famous icon of the guitar with a big 'NO' written beside it. The main door! It cannot get more public than that. Obviously the protestor was not the type who would back off.

In yet another shocking discovery, the establishment found that the same icon and slogan, now embellished with a picture of a dejected face, had appeared on the window pane of the sitting room. The campaigner is, however, tight-lipped, letting the slogans do all the talking and piling up pressure on the establishment through these increasingly loud messages while comfortably watching television or playing.

The establishment sought time to fulfill the demand. It has, as usual, adopted a wait and watch strategy to find out the extent to which the agitation would intensify and what shape it would take before the next steps are considered.

Meanwhile the lone agitator found some support on the internet and social media. Some people told me rather unpleasantly to concede to her demands.

A Peaceful Turn

In a quick change of tactics by the lone agitator (born on 2nd October incidentally), the angry and rebellious slogans gave way to a softer tone. A suggestion made to the protestor by a member of the management that a positive approach could bring positive results led to a change in approach. The NO turned into a YES and the sad face became a smiling face. The mood was one of compromise and of openness.

New Post-Its have appeared – with a 'YES' and a picture of the guitar.

One Post-It carried the image of a smiling face and heart-shaped signs of love. The Post-Its are pasted over the previous messages that were dark and sad. It was a sign that the past could now be forgotten and negotiations could be carried out in an atmosphere of love, hope and optimism.

This war was won over by love. I finally told Anjali that she could have her guitar. I found it incredible that she could change her attitude so quickly and with that, shift the entire energy of the situation leading to a favourable resolution.

My way of getting what I want is to ask for it, take a Me-versus-You position, perceive injustice at the first any sign of rejection, shut myself off and give up. Then, wonder why I do not get what I want despite my best efforts. Can I change my attitude to get what I want?

A Return Gift for You: To get what you want, hold on to your goal, but be flexible and open. Change your attitude, your approach, when things get stuck. Your ego could be the only thing that's getting in the way of what you want.

6
Heads I Win, Tails You Lose

Anjali and I had to settle an issue in a game.

"Okay, we'll toss," I said. "Whoever wins, wins."

"Okay," she said, delighted at this new game. It was a first for her.

I got the coin. Then the devil got to me.

"Heads I win," I hustled, showing her the heads. "Tails you lose."

She listened and nodded, all trust and innocence.

I paused for a moment.

"Shall I toss?" I asked again.

There was a trace of confusion on her face. Clearly she was thinking beyond 'father' and 'trust'. She did not give the go-ahead. After a moment, she spoke.

"I am comfused," she said slowly (as she mispronounced 'confused' those days). Her brow furrowed deeply as she tried to get her mind around the one thing that was bothering her.

Something was not right.

Then it hit home and her eyes opened wide.

"Then, how will I win?" She asked.

Ah. Was I glad to be caught! But seriously, you could con me with a no-win trick like that even today if an authority figure played it on me. Anjali heeded her instinct, stopped to think instead of agreeing right away, until she figured it out. Good for you Anjali. When unsure, wait.

My way of dealing with con jobs is to first avoid looking foolish at all costs, act like I know it all when in fact I do not know, and in the process, get cheated with my eyes wide open. Then, wonder how others cheat me so easily when I do not cheat anyone. Can I be smart enough to say 'I don't know', when I am not sure?

A Return Gift for You: To make the right decision in a dilemma, trust your intuition, which acts in your best interests and ignore your ego which wants you to please others at any cost. You gain when you act in your best interests, you lose when you try to please others. Many times, appearing to be foolish is a smarter option than being fooled while trying to look smart.

7. Repaying Amaan's Kindness With Interest

Anjali told me about an incident that happened at school.

"I forgot my pencil *Nanna*. So my friend Amaan gave me his pencil. It was very sharp. You know how sometimes the point breaks easily. So I was very careful. You see, Amaan gave me the pencil out of kindness. I had to use it carefully and not spoil it or anything right?"

I nodded and smiled at her.

I wish I could think that way about this world too. That there is immense kindness and love around us, and whatever we get, we must use carefully and give it back. If I take from the environment can I use it and give it back with care? If I receive love and kindness from a person, can I give what I took and more?

Why abuse the gifts we receive?

My way of repaying the kindness I receive is to grab it with both hands, use it carelessly, apologize for damages (sometimes not even that) and walk away. Then wonder why people are not so kind to me anymore. Can I be less selfish, greedy and careless just because it's not mine?

A Return Gift for You: You could open up a bigger pipeline for giving and receiving when you handle life's gifts with love and care, as if they were your own. If possible, give back a little more than you receive.

8
I Have a Role to Play

A bad cold and a disturbed night made Anjali sleepy and cranky in the morning. We told her she could take the day off and rest. But she woke up in a couple of hours and declared – "I want to go to school."

It was two hours past the school timing. So I told her I'd call and find out if she could go. "Why call? I want to go," she said. Luckily, her teachers had no problem with that.

On the way to school I asked her why she wanted to go when she was unwell.

"But if I don't go who will speak my lines?" She shot back.

"What lines?" I asked.

"For the presentation," she said.

Anjali's class had a presentation coming up in a couple of days. It was a small event but she felt it was her duty to go and speak her lines, because if she did not, who would? Her class depended on her.

What a lovely team it would be if all members thought in such terms and showed up for the team even in illness. How many times do I go to deliver my lines for my team in spite of physical discomfort?

I did not understand the import of her act as fully as her teacher and classmates did.

"They all clapped for me when I showed up in class," said Anjali, smiling sheepishly, when she came back that evening. "I did not understand why they were clapping." Young lady, it does not matter as long as you did what you felt had to be done.

My approach to being a smart member of the team is to first take a Team-versus-Me stand, ask what the team has done for me and give only as much as I receive because it is not smart to work more than required. Then, wonder why I'm not part of winning teams. Can I identify with my team fully, and give it all I have?

A Return Gift for You: To benefit from the synergistic, collective effort of your team, contribute wholeheartedly to your team in your own best interests. You win when your team wins, you lose when it loses, so give your best. Hold nothing back.

9
So, You Call!

"No one's calling me," I complained to Anjali. "No one loves me."

She looked at me.

"So you call *na*," she said. "Then you can speak to them and feel happy. Why wait for them?"

Simple as that, huh? Okay, let me try.

My method of reaching out for love and affection is to stare at my phone expectantly, get mad that the other person is not calling, stew inside and work myself into a state so that by the time they call me I am ready to snap at them. Then, wonder why no one reaches out to me when I need them. Can I act first instead of waiting?

A Return Gift for You: You simplify life many times over when you act in favour of what YOU want. Do not wait for people to understand your need and come to you to fulfill your secret desires. Take responsibility for what you want and you will not be disappointed. Reach out, now.

10
A Gift From ME to ME

Anjali wanted to buy herself a gift on Children's Day. I gave her a budget of Rs. 100. (She hates my budgeting tactics and tells me – "Give me money from my bank account. I want to buy with my own money.")

She chose to buy for herself, of all things, a fountain pen. It came with a bottle of ink and an ink dropper. Since we were getting the other gifts we had bought wrapped, Anjali said "I want my gift to be wrapped too." We were amused and so were the girls at the gift wrapping section.

Anjali waited patiently while the attendants wrapped her gift. They gave it to her with a smile, but minus the card. She handed them a card and had that put on the gift.

Then she wrote on it - *From Anjali to Anjali*. And only then, did she gift herself the pen.

It's a fine attitude to treat yourself as the most special person in your life. I need to learn this quickly.

My way of treating myself well is to plan a good gift for myself, then doubt if I deserve it and end up buying myself something inconsequential because I don't really matter – even to myself. Then, wonder why I do not matter to the world. Can I give myself the best I can give myself - from Hari to Hari?

A Return Gift for You: If you build your most special relationship with yourself, you can't go wrong. Get yourself fully on your own side. Support yourself. It could change the quality of all your relationships. Treat yourself best.

Stop Cheating the Bees

"How do we get honey *Nanna*?" Asked Anjali.

"From the beehive," I said. "But you have to drive the bees away from the beehive. Or else they will sting you."

"So how do they drive them away?" She asked.

I recalled the one time I saw people doing that. "They light a fire under the hive and drive the bees away. Then they get the hive and take the honey from it."

Anjali was indignant when she heard that.

"But that's so unfair. You drive away someone from their home and then steal their stuff?"

It is, isn't it? It's criminal. But we seem to be doing that all the time. Especially to nature. Our idea of progress and business seems to thrive on this principle. Rob. Steal. Exploit. Take what belongs to you without compunction.

But there's a way, as the Taoists say, that is ideal for making a living. Live like the bee, which does not hurt the flower when it takes its honey. The elegant way is to do things without hurting anyone and in such a way that everyone benefits.

My way of making a livelihood is to find someone who has something of value for me, someone kind, gullible and soft and exploit their goodness and resources fully without ever thinking of a scenario where we all benefit. Then, wonder why all my resources have dried up. Can I be more creative, sensitive and and less greedy in my choices?

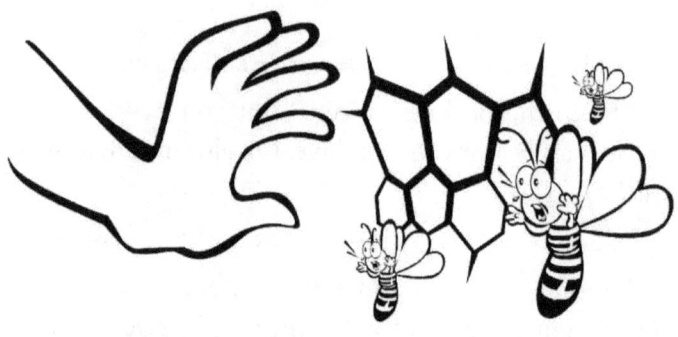

A Return Gift for You: You will find greater peace, more abundance and support from the environment if you look for solutions that benefit all stakeholders – especially those from whom you take. You can create much more together when all your stakeholders are on the same side, not against each other. Think win-win.

12
We Didn't Discover The Zero

Anjali and I were playing cricket one day. I asked her what her score was. She was in a mischievous mood and announced loudly that she was batting on zero and did a couple of goofy jigs to celebrate her accomplishment. Then suddenly she turned to me and asked – "We Indians only discovered the zero na *Nanna*!" She'd read about the 'inventing zero' fact in a book. I nodded. She celebrated some more.

After continuing in the same vein for a while, she stopped abruptly again.

"But we did not really discover the zero did we? People in the olden times discovered it. You didn't discover it *Nanna*? I didn't. So why are we dancing?"

Ah, I cannot tell you how much I agree this line of thought. When I see people taking credit for the zero, the Vedas, yoga, our culture and for almost everything in this world, I think the same. Agreed, someone did do their job well then. But what are we doing to take it further?

My way of contributing to society is to identify great work done in the past, interpret their work to suit my own agenda and cover myself with glory. Then, wonder why no one's recognizing my contribution. Can I stop leaning on others and stand on my own?

🎁 **A Return Gift for You:** You could create your own unique contribution by taking inspiration from the past, not by basking in reflected glory. Find your own song.

13
I Don't Care If Michael Jackson Is Black or White

I was watching a music video of 'Thriller' by Michael Jackson. Anjali joined me.

"Oh, he looks different," she said. "I saw him in another video and he looked different there."

I jumped in, eager to educate her. "You know we used to watch this video many times when we were young. This was his greatest album. He really changed our lives." Anjali was watching his moves intently. I felt the need to add some more.

"He was black then. Then he changed the colour of his skin and became white. I preferred him when he was black. There was nothing wrong with him as he was right?" I said.

"I don't care if he is black or white," she replied. "All I want to see is how well he dances and sings."

She moonwalked herself out of the room.

That ended that particular conversation on colour and discrimination. It's still discrimination if I choose one over the other.

My way of dealing with discrimination is to first discriminate from my perspective, then discriminate against other discriminators and feel superior in my discrimination.

Then, wonder why they are all so biased. Can I be secure enough to let things be as they are without wanting to change them?

A Return Gift for You: You could save much of your time and energy by not getting stuck in discriminating – for or against. When you accept all things in their unique nature, you progress faster and enjoy the many shades of life.

14. Let Them Do Their Job, You Do Yours

A couple of Bollywood stars were dancing to a popular song on TV. They gyrated, twisted and contorted with great energy.

"Why are they dancing like mad people?" I asked Anjali, an avid Bollywood fan. She was watching the performance without blinking an eye.

"Let them do their job," she said. "You do your job."

I guess I could. I had no business there really.

I really believe that the recipe for greater efficiency is just that - I do my job and let others do theirs. We could save much time and energy by doing our job well instead of watching others and telling them how to do their job. The young lady seems to have got the hang of it.

My way of adding efficiency to society is to find ways to better everyone else's life, while my life is languishing. Then, wonder why there are no takers for my advice. Can I be aware that when I speak of others' work, I am not doing mine?

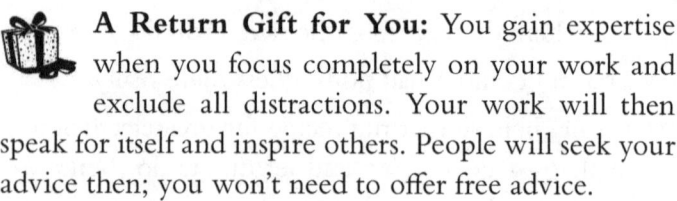 **A Return Gift for You:** You gain expertise when you focus completely on your work and exclude all distractions. Your work will then speak for itself and inspire others. People will seek your advice then; you won't need to offer free advice.

15 Hand-written Letters and Land Line Phones

I took Anjali to the post office to explain how it works. She liked the idea of writing letters and wrote to her cousins. Her letters were adorned with pictures, stickers, I-love-yous and several large hearts. Her cousins replied with matching letters.

One day she accosted me with an envelope. She had written a letter to her *ajoba* (her grandfather) and wanted me to post it. I called him for his address – I realized I didn't have anyone's address with me anymore. He was thrilled with the idea of receiving a letter from his seven-year-old granddaughter and started preparing his reply to her. He started off telling me his opening lines on the phone itself. There was excitement in the air. About a letter?

Another thing at home with very little use (like the letter box) is the landline phone. We get an average of two calls a month on it. I told Anjali that since she does not have a phone of her own, that landline phone could be hers. She was thrilled with the idea of owning a phone. She wrote down the numbers of her aunts, cousins and grandparents and called them daily. She took over the old phone book, mostly fixed-line numbers. Her relatives were happy at this new development and they too called her on the same line. Suddenly the phone was ringing a lot more and talk was abundant in the house. It felt like an old joint family has awakened.

It's interesting, how Anjali added a new life to the hand-written letters and the landline. How did these forgotten and uncool things come alive?

My way of dealing with 'cool' and 'uncool' things is to keep the 'uncool things' hidden away because it's not cool to be seen with them anymore, but not get rid of them either because I cannot let them go. Then, wonder what I am doing with this old love of mine that's hidden in the attic. Can I stop branding things as 'cool' or 'uncool'?

A Return Gift for You: You could change the quality of your relationships if you drop popular perspectives and stay honest to your own. You could enjoy a greater choice in all aspects of life instead of picking and choosing from someone else's limited wish list.

16
Be Good To Yourself First

I was having a long, heated discussion on the phone. After I disconnected, Anjali asked me who it was. I told her that it was a school where I'd conducted a writing workshop.

"They are not paying me on time as they promised," I said.

Her expression changed. She said in utmost surprise. "But that's not fair."

I was impressed by her spontaneous reaction.

"They should pay you *na Nanna*. You did their work. If Lakshmi (our maid) came and asked for money after doing all the work and *Mamma* said she wouldn't pay, how will it be? If they do not pay you, go to the police and tell them."

So simple.

I wonder why I stopped thinking like that. I am more concerned with keeping the peace and putting up with the other party even if they are dishonouring the terms of agreement. Each time I compromise a little more. I become lesser and lesser.

What was the number to call the police again?

My way of valuing my work is to deliver good work, doubt if it is good enough, suffer needless mental trauma over it and seed my doubt in my client's mind. Then, wonder why my client does not see value in my work. Can I value myself and my work highly, irrespective of the work I do?

A Return Gift for You: You can change the way others value your work when you value it yourself. When you take pride in your work, you take greater responsibility for it. That makes the quality of your work better. Value your work and yourself first.

17
Throw Those Candies *Nanna!*

The traffic was at standstill at the traffic signal. While waiting I spotted this small kid, seven or eight years old perhaps, tapping on car windows and begging for alms. He was one of those kids with a spring in his step and an endearing smile on his grimy face. I reached for the candy in my dashboard and waited for him to approach our car. I was hoping to give him some candy. But before he could come to our car, the signal changed and the traffic started moving.

The kid turned and ran to his mother who was sitting on the lawns with a small baby. I hoped to catch his eye as I passed him so I could give him the candy. But the traffic picked up speed and we passed him, candy still in hand. Too bad, I thought.

I was putting the candy away, when I heard Anjali from the rear seat.

"If it was me, I'd have thrown the candy on the grass. He'd have loved to catch them."

She was right. Here I was more concerned about the appropriateness of my act than what was important in the situation, which is the intent. I wish I'd thrown the candy. It would have been such a lovely surprise for the young boy who'd be least bothered about propriety anyway. He would have delighted in the candy raining from the sky!

My way of being a spontaneous person is to worry about being appropriate (when not required) and not being appropriate (when required) and finally not being both. Then, wonder why my spontaneity is not flowing easily. Can I worry less about others' reactions to my actions and more about the spontaneity of my own actions?

A Return Gift for You: When in doubt, choose in favour of your actions over other people's reactions. Be spontaneous. You will find yourself in a better space. More of the authentic 'you' will emerge. Go for it!

18
The Dog Protests

All kids go through a dog phase they say and Anjali went through one too. Sadly for her, Shobha and I are not really dog people or pet people (and sometimes I suspect, not even human people). But Anjali loves animals and has steadily progressed from hamsters (no), kitten (no), rabbits (no) and fish (yes), to dogs. The two goldfish, Tutty and Fruity, went to their fish heaven after a short stay with us. Anjali was distressed at their early departure and the pet story stopped there.

But not for long. Anjali's first request for a dog caused a flutter at home.

"I don't have a brother," she announced sadly. I looked at her. How can we get her a brother now?

"At least if I had a dog, then I would not be lonely," she added. I nodded.

"Can I have a dog?" She asked me directly, after seeing that the conversation was going nowhere.

Pushed into a corner I responded with a decisive, "Let's see," before reeling off my reasons why a dog might not be a good idea. Most of them on the lines of, who will take care of it, because certainly I won't. (I have to take care of myself.)

"I will take care of it *Nanna*," she said, all serious with good intentions, and meaning it wholeheartedly. "I will take it for walks, I will bathe it, feed it." I nodded.

"Yay!" She yelled. "*Nanna* has agreed."

I had not. I had merely nodded.

Shobha was far less diplomatic and informed Anjali that she was not convinced with the need for a dog. "Full time care, no vacations and so on and so forth." The dog idea stopped right there.

I thought Anjali would give up. But the young lady was made of different stuff. For every objection we raised, she Googled answers. What to do with dogs when on vacation? What to feed dogs? How to train dogs? How to maintain dogs? What types of dogs are safe for

children? Printouts started piling up on my table with answers to all our doubts.

"I want a golden retriever," she said one day. "How much does it cost?"

I had no clue. "Maybe 15,000-20,000," I said. Everything costs that much these days. She was surprised they cost that much. She googled the price of a golden retriever.

"It costs Rs. 1200," she said.

It was my turn to be surprised. I checked. Turned out the one she had found was a stuffed toy. The real ones were more expensive. Anjali and I looked at the prices in dismay.

"Don't worry about the price," I said looking at her crestfallen face. "It's more about the responsibility. We cannot bring it home and leave it alone after we get tired of it. It will be a part of the family for the next 13-14 years."

"12 years," she corrected me. She had researched on how long golden retrievers live.

"Dog," she points, to every dog she sees. I squirm.

Her screen saver on the computer is a golden retriever. In her things-to-do list 'Getting a Dog' is prominent. Her folder is full of dog pictures and stories. She learned the names of the various breeds by heart. She knows their behaviour, how long they live and the diseases they are likely to get. She compiled an article about kennels and dog food. The dogs have been named in anticipation – Jumpy when it is small and Bruno when big. How not to confuse dogs by naming them too many times was also discussed. At the super market she pointed to Pedigree and Drools and said she would feed her dog that. A packet of Pedigree has been bought to feed stray dogs on the road. At night before she slept she told me her daily routine when dog comes — walk dog, feed dog, play with dog, train dog. I will teach dog to fetch she says. When she got emotional, she said she will get her dog when she turns 18, with her own money - when she is in America. This killed me a bit.

A cute stuffed toy appeared on my table. A hint?

A piggy bank appeared on my desk with a Post-It stuck on it. The Post-It says "Golden Retriever" and "Rs. 25,000." The fund has already raised a few hundreds. The piggy too has a suitably sad expression on its face.

As a backup, Anjali has researched that one could adopt dogs for free. She has found the many benefits of adopting dogs. Chiefly, for me – 'they are for free.'

The Legal Route

The Memorandum of Understanding

Anjali prepared a document titled 'I really want a dog' and left it on my desk. She typed it (all 400 words), addressed directly to me and her *Mamma*, telling us why she wants a dog and how she would take care of it. At the bottom was a direct instruction – Answer 'Yes' or 'No'. There was space for *Mamma* to write her suggestions and then space for me. Both copies were left on the desk. Where did she get the idea to get our signatures on that paper I wonder? Everyday she asked – "have you written Yes or No with your suggestion on the letter?" I think I better. I couldn't deal with this pressure.

The Contract

After the MoU episode, Anjali went ahead and drafted a proper CONTRACT! I suspect she might have stumbled upon a kiddies website that has a step-by-step procedure for children on how to coax parents into getting them dogs. The contract talks of how 'we' are all involved in taking care of the dog and whose responsibility is what. When this whole affair became an 'us' thing I don't know but now it appears that I am an active party to getting a dog — which I am not. There are signature spaces for parents and for her too. I signed. I don't know why. I think I will leave it to Shobha to handle this.

One thing I know for sure — whoever Anjali chooses to like or love is one lucky dog. She pulls out all stops for them.

My way of getting what I want is to ask for it tentatively, withdraw at the first sign of resistance, resent all parties concerned for raising doubts and never ask again to punish myself, and them. Then, I wonder why I am suffering and they are not. Can I be wholehearted in my effort to get what I want?

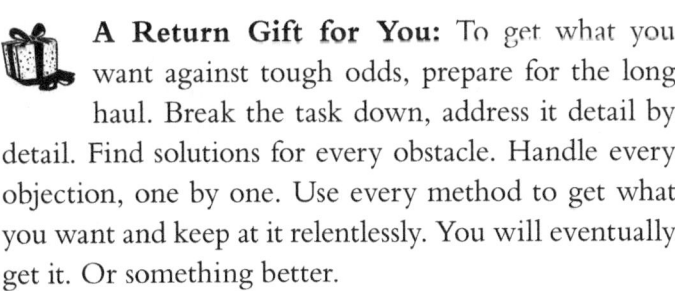 **A Return Gift for You:** To get what you want against tough odds, prepare for the long haul. Break the task down, address it detail by detail. Find solutions for every obstacle. Handle every objection, one by one. Use every method to get what you want and keep at it relentlessly. You will eventually get it. Or something better.

19
Give Up My Subsidy – Now

We were driving to the airport when eight-year-old Anjali spotted a large hoarding that said – Give up your LPG subsidy.

"What is subsidy *Nanna*?" She asked.

I first explained what LPG is, then what a subsidy is, why it is subsidized and why the government wants those who can afford it to give up the subsidy. I don't know how much of it she understood but she got one thing spot on – we belonged to the group of people who could afford it and were still claiming the subsidy.

"Let us give up our subsidy *Nanna*," she said in that urgent manner of hers. "Today."

I asked her why.

"So the poor can benefit. We can do our bit for them. We can afford it."

By now she was very animated.

I gave her an alternative. "What if I gave you the subsidy amount to spend on the poor the way you want to?"

"No," she said firmly. "Let us give up the subsidy."

She had also noticed that there was a website called giveupmysubsidy.com. She asked me to visit that site and checked every other day whether I really did give up our subsidy.

LPG, subsidy, government, poverty – how does she understand this? But she seems to know one thing – that by our giving up something, someone else may benefit.

Giving up my subsidy seems like the right thing to do. I am glad for that hoarding, that idea of seeking public participation by some trusting soul, glad that it caught the eye of a child in a car driving past. Sometimes that is all we require – an honest effort. It can connect anywhere, anytime.

My reaction to any small sacrifice asked of me for public good is to withdraw instantly, be suspicious of the scheme, stay convinced that all else may benefit at my cost and reject the idea. Then, wonder why the spirit of sacrifice is missing in society. Can I stop being so petty and think of the bigger picture?

A Return Gift for You: When you give, you open yourself up to receive, possibly bigger things. Give wholeheartedly knowing better things are in store for you. Giving frees you.

Plucking and Praying

Anjali and I were walking around in the colony. She pointed to a tree on our path.

"Look at those flowers *Nanna*," she said. "They are so high up."

It was a *Nandivardhanam* tree. I told her that people pluck the white flowers from the tree for their daily prayers. The flowers on the lower branches were missing because the praying population of the colony can pluck those easily. The flowers on the higher branches were spared because the devout could not reach them.

Anjali was not amused.

"First they disappoint God by plucking flowers that God made. Then they use the same flowers to pray to God. What will God think?"

Yes. What will God think? Does anyone care about what God thinks?

My way of relating to God is to fight violently to get his grace, show no love or compassion for others and step all over them in the race to get God's blessings for me and my family, and no one else. Then, I wonder why God is not being kind to us. Can I stop worrying that God will stop taking care of me?

A Return Gift for You: When you choose to follow the spirit of things, you act from a space of love and compassion. You do not need anything else. Love is God. And vice versa.

An Interview with a Four-Year-old

Anjali turned four and I decided to interview her. I asked her if I could. She agreed and suggested that it might be a good idea if we sat on the sofa in the living room where it would be more comfortable than my room. Once there, we started.

Me: What do you like most?
Anjali: (After some doubt whether it included all sorts of things) Banana.

Me: What do you like doing the most?
Anjali: Jumping from high places. (Her favourite pastime is jumping from the sofa these days).

Me: Who do you like playing with the most?
Anjali: Mansi. (Her best friend from school)

Me: What do you play with her?
Anjali: Who will eat fast.

Me: What games do you like?
Anjali: We love opening buttons and shutting buttons fast.

Me: Do you like books?
Anjali: Yeah.

Me: Which ones?
Anjali: Pepper.

Me: Who are your favourite cartoon characters?
Anjali: Nobita (from Doraemon)

Me: Why?
Anjali: Because he always does things. So funny.

Me: Do you like laughing?
Anjali (nodding): Also everyone smiles and they also laugh.

Me: Crying?
Anjali: Then everyone starts crying. I don't feel good when they cry.

Me: What is your favourite food?
Anjali: Chicken biryani, rice and chips. Ice creams, but I am afraid I'll get a cold.

Me: Do you like your school?
Anjali: Yes.

Me: Why?

Anjali: Because they put all happy designs and all that. That's why I love the school. I love playing in my school with my friends.

Me: What songs do you like?

Anjali: 'Gardener plants a seed.' Maybe, 'There's a rainbow in the sky' as well.

Me: Your favourite movies?

Anjali: Nemo, Lion King… Pooh.

Me: Why?

Anjali: Because they are so funny. Nemo is not listening to his father.

Me: What do you like doing at home?

Anjali: Pretending to be a fairy with my Mom and Dad. Playing with my Mom and Dad.

Me: Anything else that you would like to have?

Anjali (confirming): What we don't have at home? Maybe a Barbie doll (she has some six). Or maybe playing cards.

Me: What do you think of your *Nanna*?

Anjali: I think I love my Daddy. Because he does not shout at me. He gives me everything.

Me: What do you think of *Mamma*?

Anjali: She gives me all whatever I want for breakfast and lunch. She cooks whatever I ask her. And whatever I want she gives it to me. I love my Mom too.

Me: What do you think your Dad does?

Anjali: Work. On the computer. Typing.

Me: And what do you think your Mom does?

Anjali: Work. With her aunties.

Me: Who loves you most in class?

Anjali: Mansi. We both love each other.

Me: What do you think of life?

Anjali: Life? I don't know.

Anjali asked if she could interview me. I said she could. Now that she had the hang of things Anjali asked me a question.

Anjali: If you are scared, what do you do?

Me: (not knowing what to answer) Perhaps I will try to look at what is it that is scaring me a bit more closely. Maybe it is not so scary at all. But if it is still scary, I get scared.

She nodded and ended this rather short interview.

PART 2

HOW TO BE HAPPY AND HOW TO LOVE AND BE LOVED

21
The Secret to a Happy World

We were driving home late at night. I heard Anjali speaking softly to herself as she hugged her doll. "I am happy, *Nanna* is happy, *Mamma* is happy, *Ajji* is happy, *Baba* is happy... we are all happy," she chanted, looking at the night sky. It was an unending list of all the people in her world – aunts, uncles, cousins, teachers, friends, maids, ayahs, watchmen, dolls, cousin's dog and others. She caught me eavesdropping, smiled, and continued with her affirmations for happiness.

I remembered a self-help workshop I attended many moons ago. The facilitator taught us how to use positive affirmations to change our thoughts and beliefs. Since our thoughts are creative, she said, we can create by focusing on what we think. (I rejected the idea immediately – I am a great rejecter). Life can't be as simple as that, I declared. We cannot change our lives so easily. Moreover, happy thoughts are difficult to create. I was happier with my unhappy thoughts.

What Anjali was saying sounded like those positive affirmations. Has she been secretly attending self-help workshops for three-year-olds? The tense was right (present tense), the words perfect (focus on what you want), the feelings spot on (as if she was living it now). I had struggled to construct even one positive affirmation properly in that workshop. How was Anjali getting it so right?

If her affirmations were one thing, the trouble she took to include everyone she could remember and make them 'happy', was quite another. With her thoughts she was creating her world of happiness lovingly, meticulously, instead of waiting for others to do something about it first. The thought that someone was making my world happy made me feel happy.

My ways of contributing to happiness in the world is to first check if the world is doing anything to make me happy, feel unhappy that others are happier than I am, and resign myself to a life of unhappiness. Then, I wonder who can make me happy in this whole wide world. Can I stop holding others responsible for my happiness?

A Return Gift for You: You could choose to create happiness for yourself and others if you take responsibility for it. You can give up your dependence on others to give you happiness. Your happiness is within. Unlock it.

22
To Get Loads of Love, Expect It Everywhere

Shobha and I were planning a trip to Pune. Anjali overheard us.

"Let's go soon," she said. "My *Ajji* (grandmother) is waiting for me." She kept that enthusiasm going until we reached Pune a couple of days later.

At Pune, Anjali raced off to her *Ajji* screaming '*Ajji*'. We told her about Anjali's drama. *Ajji* loved it. (She loves Hindi and Marathi serials too). She gave her grandchild lots of toys to play and food to eat.

Ajji done with, Anjali's focus shifted to her cousins. "Pooja is waiting for me," and then "Prarthana is waiting for me," and "Miskil is waiting for me." The whole world was waiting for her it seemed and she completely believed that. When the young ladies in question were told about how much Anjali believed that they were all waiting for her, they were thrilled.

Anjali did not stop for a moment to think if the world loves her as much as she loves the world. She had no doubt. She knew. She expected and demanded love, and behaved as if love was waiting for her in the most unlikely of people – like me for instance. Whenever she comes with that huge expectation of love, I am forced to search deep inside to find it and am pleasantly surprised to find it there.

For me, even if love was handed on a platter, I'd doubt it. I just don't believe I am good enough for unconditional love to wait for me. I wait for proof and even more proof. I'm smart you see.

My way of getting love from the world is to send out a strong 'I-am-not-sure-if-you-would-like-me' vibe, doubt if anyone would find me loveable and expect a weak reception anyway. Then, I wonder why the world is not showering me with love. Can I believe that the world is waiting for me with all its love, wherever I go?

A Return Gift for You: You could find love everywhere if you expect it – without conditions and without doubt. You will always find what you look for in the end – love or disappointment.

23
There's Peace in War

Anjali pestered me to buy her a chess board. Then she pestered me to teach her how to play. She was an eager student and soon learned how to place the pieces and move them. The knights caused some problems initially with their unpredictable moves. But she kept her interest going and learned enough to play a few games with me.

But whenever she played, I could sense her distress. She was clearly dismayed at the deceit and planning that goes on in a game of chess. For an almost-four-year-old, life must be pretty simple, fun and straightforward. Everything chess was not.

I did not realize how much she disagreed with the philosophy of the game until I saw her playing with her Chitra *maushi* one day. "Look *Nanna*," said Anjali happily. "No fighting in this chess. They are all friends here." I observed the new developments in her game. In Anjali's version, all the pieces were mingling about amicably in a display of friendship that's rarely seen on the chess board. The white king was riding a black rook and was heading out for a jaunt, white knights seemed to be escorting the black queen for some sightseeing, and the bishops were counseling some errant pawns. It was a big party out there with no sign of war.

There was little doubt as to which version of the game she preferred. Having discovered a harmonious way to play the game of chess, Anjali's face glowed with pleasure. I suspect that is how we were originally made, seeking harmony, fun and helping one another. And then we had to grow up and invent deceit, cunning and warfare.

My way of playing a game is to convert the game into a war, opponents into enemies and twist the conditions to suit my end. Then, I wonder why everyone is hostile to me. Can I compete without ego?

A Return Gift for You: When you seek harmony, you can collaborate with your opponents and achieve far more together, far more easily. You can find excitement in growth through collaboration, rather than acquisition.

24 To Get More Love, Love More People

"I love only you Anjali," I declared loudly. "I love only you in this whole world."

She was distressed at my obvious lack of understanding of how it all works. She told me patiently that I must not love her alone.

"You must love everyone *Nanna*. Otherwise people won't love you."

To drive home her point she said, "See, I love you but I love everybody else also *na*. I love *Mamma, Mythily attha, Mansi, Chimu, Baba* (and a long list of others) ...also. Like that you must also love everyone."

I acted like I got it, and after a while, told her again that I love only her. With hands on her hips she told me. *"Arre,* how many times should I tell you *Nanna.* You must love everyone."

You can tell by her concern that she really believes I might lose out on this wisdom and remain unloved.

My way of getting myself more love is to love my family and my friends only and no one else (at times not even them), but expect the whole world to reach out and love me. Then, wonder why there's not enough love in my life. Can I love everyone?

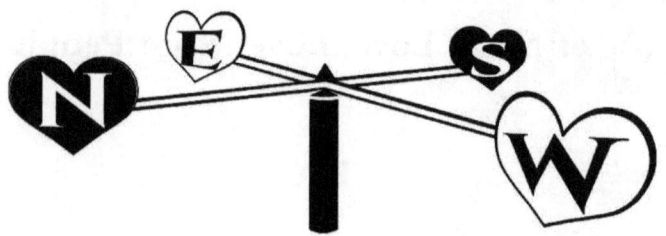

A Return Gift for You: You can access all the love you want if you remove your prejudices, fears and conditions. You can enjoy the free flowing channel of love. With love there is nothing to fear; love is the opposite of fear.

25
The Magic Wand of Happiness

I asked Anjali the secret of happiness. She smiled and batted her eyelashes. That simple huh? Smile and bat your eyelashes. The secret of happiness!

Anjali and the magic wand going to a Halloween party

I got busy after that enlightening conversation and was watching television. She popped up in front of me and waved a wand at me. I asked her to move aside. "You're blocking my view." I said.

"But *Nanna*," she said, miffed. "I am making you happy with my magic wand."

Making me happy? How can you? How can anybody?

"*Mamma* told me that I can do anything with my magic wand so I decided to make you and *Mamma* happy with this magic wand."

Now that was a very nice thought indeed and most unexpected. But why was she thinking of making us happy instead of asking things for herself?

I smiled indulgently, secretly disbelieving Anjali's magic wand and its powers. How can it make me happy? I was quite happy with my unhappiness. Who are these happy wand makers? Fakes, Frauds.

But what mattered was that Anjali believed in her magic wand and got the result she wanted. She put a smile on my face didn't she? What else do I want? Happiness guaranteed for a lifetime?

My way of making people happy is to ignore the obvious and natural ways (like smiling at people), and explore complicated and obscure ways that make happiness a boring, metaphysical concept. Then, wonder why there are no magic moments in my life. Can I stop doubting and start receiving?

A Return Gift for You: You experience magic, when you believe in it. The world is only what we believe it to be. Belief leads to experience. Not the other way round. Believe.

26
You Can Be Happy When You Win

Anjali and I played a card game. It's called *bhikhar-sahukar* in Marathi which translates into rich man-poor man because the game eventually makes one rich and the other poor. We divide cards, throw cards alternately and the one who throws a card that matches the previous card takes the loot.

Anjali began by pointing out how I normally don't win in games against her. (How did she know?) Much to her surprise and mine, I started winning heavily. "Wow," she said. "You won *Nanna*." I shrugged nonchalantly as if it didn't matter to me, hoping to make it easier on her. She was pretty severe on that reaction of mine.

"So be happy!" She said. "You won." I nodded sheepishly.

My winning streak continued. I found myself getting more and more uncomfortable with each win. Sensing my discomfort she once again pointed out what was missing in my approach. "Be happy *na*?" She said. Soon, Anjali lost all her cards. She did not cry or feel sad at losing. She reacted differently.

"Now you have to give me half of your cards," she said simply. "That's the rule. We must share if one of us gets everything and the other person loses everything."

I shared, as per her new rules, and the game continued. "It's more fun this way," she said. "The game never ends."

"But the game ends when you lose all your cards," I explained, eager to drive home the fact that I had indeed won and that she had lost and that the game was over. Hullo? One must lose so another wins you see. Everyone cannot win can they?

My explanation made no impression on her.

"But I play like that," she said. And that was that.

In retrospect it's not a bad way to look at a game or life. The game never ends for us if we choose to look win-win. There is enough and more for all if we look beyond winning for ourselves, are flexible, and can seek help. Everyone helps everyone, everyone is happy. Winning is an attitude.

My approach to handling winning is to be uncomfortable with the responsibility of being a winner, wonder if I really deserve to win, view my victory as an end in itself, take it for granted and lose what I gained just as quickly. Then, wonder why I don't win much despite trying so hard. Can I just enjoy the good in the moment and not analyze the why and how?

 A Return Gift for You: You could accept your victory without guilt, and your loss without shame. You win both ways then.

27 And Remember… Everyone Loves You

I was pulling Anjali's leg again.

"No one called me today," I complained.

"So?" she asked.

"No one is thinking about me," I said.

"Maybe they are thinking about you but not calling," she said.

"Nobody loves me," I said putting on a sad face.

She looked at me. Now what, she seemed to say.

"But I love you *Nanna*," she said after a moment.

"Only you love me," I whined.

"*Mamma* also loves you," she said.

"She didn't tell me so," I protested.

"That's okay. She loves you. I know," she said.

"Only the two of you love me," I continued.

"Your *Mamma* and *Nanna* also love you," she said.

"But they're dead," I said.

"Yeah, but they still love you *na*, wherever they are," she said.

Now that's a nice thought. Where did that come from?

And before I could continue with my drama she wound it up.

"And all your brothers and sisters and friends and all the people you know love you from wherever they are. Okay?" She said quickly and concluded.

That's comforting. I nodded. She nodded back.

My way of measuring the flow of love into my life is to compare the inflow of love I get with the outflow of love from me, perceive unfairness in the transaction, reduce my outflow commensurately, and soon discover that whatever little flow was coming my way had dried up as well. Then, wonder why the world does not love me anymore. Can I be assured that I there is an abundance of love that is coming my way at all times whether it is said or not?

A Return Gift for You: You are connected to all the love in the world. All you have to do is to tune in and receive it. If you're not receiving it, you are either out of tune or you are blocking it from coming to you. Open up and receive.

28 Thanks for Digging the Road, Guys

I was driving through a narrow lane that had been freshly dug up for pipeline work. I made familiar faces and noises and expressed my disgust at the bad planning, inefficiency and bad governance.

Anjali chose to see it all differently.

"But they are digging for us only na *Nanna*," she piped up.

That's true. Why don't I think of that?

Every time there's work happening on the road, it is for us. Whether it is a pipeline, a metro line or road-widening, it is for us. Then why do I complain so much about every little thing? When will I understand that everything that's happening in my world is happening for me and not against me?

My way of dealing with anything that upsets status quo is to condemn it, make those responsible for the work into aggressors, make myself the helpless victim, and totally miss the gift in it. Then, wonder why life is so unfair to me. Can I stop fighting life at every step?

A Return Gift for You: When you view life as working 'for' you and not 'against' you, you find the gift in everything. You find that every obstacle is actually a step forward for you. Any changes to your *status quo* indicate growth. See(k) the gift everywhere.

29
We Can Build It Again

Anjali's favourite pastime those days was building sandcastles. Every other day we carried her beach set (plastic shovels, buckets etc) to the sandpit in our neighbourhood park. My job was to assist her in building sandcastles.

I deployed my extensive knowledge of sandcastle architecture and impressed her. First, I formed square blocks of sand and then dig up moats all around. Security is most important you see! My job done, I told her to stick flags, build bridges, decorate the castle and so on. She headed off in search of suitable items like a leaf, a twig or a bottle crown and decorated the castle with great care and love. The entire process took an hour sometimes.

After one such effort we sat back to admire our masterpiece.

After a couple of moments, Anjali slid her foot out and crashed one part of the castle. What was she up to? Then another part came crashing down. In minutes, our castle was flattened.

I asked her why she knocked the castle down. "We'll build it again," she said simply.

No attachment. No need for appreciation. No beating on the chest. Just a wonderful consciousness of knowing that you can build it again.

My approach to creating my masterpiece starts with announcing the big idea, then take myself and my idea too seriously, push my creation hard in case the world misses it, stew over the lukewarm response and stop creating. Then, wonder why the world does not recognize great creators like me. Can I just knock down all I built and say – 'I can do it again'?

A Return Gift for You: To do your best work, drop your attachment to it. When you are ready to let go of your creation, you can create bigger and better work. Creative work energizes, it does not deplete.

30 Can't Promise if I'll Love You in Future

In a quiet moment with the young lady, I asked – "Anjali, when you grow up, will you fight with me?"

I expected her to say that she would never fight with me and that she would love me forever and all that.

But she took a surprisingly philosophical view of the question.

"We don't know what will happen in the future *na*?" She said very practically. "We only know what happened in the past. So I cannot say if I will fight with you or not. I may or I may not. So what is there? Okay, now let us play."

That does make immense sense. Stay with the present.

My way of working on building great relationships for the future is to develop a set of narrow and rigid scenarios about people and situations, take up needless positions, and then get badly stuck inside them. Then, wonder why my relationships are not flowing easily. Can I stop trying to control things and let them be?

🎁 **A Return Gift for You:** You could enjoy love in all its hues if you allow it to flow naturally instead of trying to control it. Love charts a much better course on its own than you could ever imagine.

The Sentimental Saga of Rickety Lifts

We had to ride up to the seventh floor and took the old rickety lift. It made ominous noises as it rocked along heavenward. As soon as we got off the contraption safely, Anjali remarked that it was very nice of the elevator to take us wherever we wanted to go. I certainly never viewed elevators as helping angels taking us to our destinations. That's their job! Whenever I thought of them (which was rarely of course), I normally made critical observations about how slow they were, how badly maintained and so on. So it was a different perspective to view elevators as silent (and some not so silent of course), helpful associates of ours.

"I love lifts," she said, looking on with great love as the elevator clanked its way about, transporting some helpless soul to his destination.

As I watched Anjali and her unconditional love for the noisy lift I realized how I take so many things for granted in my life. How ungrateful I generally am!. The poor lift did take me up seven floors, didn't it? I'd have probably appreciated it better if I had to walk up and down!

My way of relating to the world around me is to take it for granted, miss the many conveniences it provides, criticize and find fault with everything. Then, wonder when life will ever be perfect. Can I be thankful to everything that I USE everyday?

A Return Gift for You: You could change the quality of your life by being grateful to the comforts you enjoy, the conveniences you get unconditionally from all that's around you. The computer, chair, desk, fan, light… what would you do without all of them? Be thankful for it – whenever you use something.

32
Look At What You Are Getting!

Anjali and I were carrying used dishes to the kitchen. "*Nanna*," she said, disapprovingly, "You dropped something from that dish." These days she lectures me like a headmistress.

"*Nanna*, if you drop stuff like that, *Bujji* (our maid) will have to pick it up tomorrow. No *Nanna*?" I nodded. "*Bujji* will have to sweep, clean and put it in the trash basket," she continued relentlessly. I felt guilty. My carelessness meant additional work for *Bujji*.

The conversation changed track.

"*Bujji* is so nice na *Nanna*," said Anjali. "She cleans our house everyday, sweeps the floor, washes dishes, clothes, cooks and makes tea." Anjali put in a lot of effort to remember all that *Bujji* does everyday, even stopping to think of any minor detail she might have missed. "She does so many things. I really love *Bujji*, I love her so much. Because *Bujji* comes everyday, our house is so clean." And she went on to enumerate many more things to the same effect.

Frankly, I only saw things that *Bujji* 'does not do'. In fact I am constantly waiting for her to 'not do' things so I can catch her out and get mad at her. Anjali was only seeing things that *Bujji* does. Naturally she is grateful for the comfort that *Bujji* provides us with whatever she does (however little, I may add). For Anjali it's a world full of surprises, gifts and miracles. For me it is a world full of disappointments, let-downs and betrayals. Gratitude they say is the key to getting all that one needs. The more grateful you are for what you have, the more of the same you create they say. I wonder what I am creating with my thoughts.

My way of creating a perfect life for myself is to examine microscopically all that's not perfect until imperfection becomes the only thing I can see around me. Then, wonder why my world is not perfect – and why it's gradually getting worse. Can I stop being the helpless victim?

A Return Gift for You: There's a gift for you every time you crib about someone or something. When you appreciate the gifts you get everyday, you find that your life is full of little surprises, not disappointments. Train your mind to identify the gift.

33
We Are All Verbs

Anjali learned English grammar at school and as always, applied her learning on us first.

"You are reading, *Mamma* is working and I am playing," she explained. "We are all verbs."

Frankly, I had not considered myself a verb ever.

"Even when we are just sitting or sleeping we are verbs *Nanna*," she explained gleefully, unraveling one of life's greatest mysteries to me. "Because you see, even then we are doing something *na*."

I was so relieved to hear that. Just 'being' is a verb is it? Looks like I don't need to worry about 'not doing enough' or 'not doing more'.

I can just 'be'! That's good enough for me. Aaah!

My way of 'doing' things is to 'worry' excessively about 'doing' because just 'being' is not good enough for other people, not really do anything except worry about not doing, or alternately, do a halfhearted job and feel terrible about it. Then, wonder why I am so stressed out whether I do or not do. Can I just be?

A Return Gift for You: You could just be and that's good enough. Do not worry about doing or not doing. There are no expectations to fulfill, no image to live up to, no ideal to pursue. Just be.

34 We Don't Need to Know Anything More – Go for It

I asked Anjali a question that I read in a book.

"What else do we need to know Anjali?" (To make our lives better, I suppose.)

Anjali said – "Nothing. I love it just the way it is."

Hmm. So it is. Everything is right exactly as it is. I am ready to handle whatever comes up now. I don't need to know anything more.

My way of dealing with any situation is to postpone dealing with it because there's something more I probably need to know, before I act. Then, wonder why life is passing me by, moment by moment, opportunity by opportunity, while I wait for more information, answers and assurances. Can I stop postponing life?

A Return Gift for You: You grow faster when you deal with life as it comes, with whatever you know. Life is in the now. The moment has presented itself because you are ready. Don't wait for perfection. Act now.

35. Thanks for the Power (Cut) Guys

"Ahhhh," I groaned loudly. The power had, once again, gone off without warning.

"I don't believe it," I ranted. "How can they do this?"

If I was looking for sympathy from the seven-year-old, I was in for a major disappointment.

I got a severe reprimand instead.

"Arre," said Anjali. "But they gave you power till now *na*. Why are you so unhappy?"

Yes. Why was I unhappy?

My way of dealing with the slight inconveniences I suffer at times, is to ignore the large part that went right and dwell on the small inconveniences. Then, wonder why things don't seem to work for me ever. Can I exit all of my experiences in a state of gratitude?

A Return Gift for You: Look back and see how far you have come and how many have helped you get here. You could not have made it on your own. There were so many who helped you on the way. Spare a thought for them.

36
When We're Equal, We're Happy

Anjali put in a lot of effort to make a chart for her school project. It included all sorts of plants, herbs, shrubs and trees.

"I took half an hour to cut the pictures, another half hour to paste them and another half an hour to write the names and draw pictures," she told me while on the way to school.

Shobha asked her how she'd feel if everyone else in her class brought really beautiful charts too.

Anjali pondered over the question for a while.

"What is there? We'll all feel happy when we do something nice *na*," she concluded.

Then she said.

"If we're all equal, we'll all feel happy."

Let me work this one out.

They all have the same charts. They make different patterns on them.

They all put in their effort. But the results are different.

The inequalities come in only when we judge the end result. And with inequality comes the feeling of being less than or more than which leads to unhappiness.

Where do we become unequal in life? We all have the same life. We choose to paint it with our uniquely different patterns.

We have the same time and energy. We get different results at different times in different measures for our efforts.

Why judge the effort and its results? We would be equal and happy if we do not compare, right? Ah, that's a relief.

My way of relating to any action of mine is to compare it with the actions of others, judge and label it, and by doing so, make what was an equal field until then, unequal. Then, wonder why things are not equal as before. Can I feel equal in every situation?

A Return Gift for You: When you are equal, there are myriad possibilities for happiness. Stay equal everywhere. You are as unique as the other person.

37
The Putting-Smiles-On-Strangers'-Faces Challenge

While going to school Anjali saw a couple of school buses pass by. The school children looked out of the windows and waved at us.

"You know," Anjali said. "Last year when Samaira and I were together in the bus, we used to play a game."

"What game?" I asked.

"How-to-make-people-happy," she said.

"How?" I asked.

"We waved at uncles and aunties standing on the road. They are all serious till then but when they see us waving, they smile. Whoever makes more people happy wins the game."

Wow! It sure looks like a nice game. I could try it. But who could I wave to?

"Why don't you make *me* happy?" I asked Anjali in all seriousness.

She smiled shyly.

"I was just joking," I said. "You make me the happiest person in the world."

The world is a happy place if we make the effort to wave and smile. Say Cheese!

I was about to send off an email when Anjali walked in. "Add a smiley," she said excitedly.

"It's an official mail Anjali," I told her. "I cannot add smileys."

"What are official mails?" She asked.

I told her what official mails were. She was not convinced. If a smiley could make things better why not use them in official mails too, said her piqued expression.

But you cannot smile all the time can you? Nor can you laugh? Until Anjali pointed it out that there are no rules against it.

My world is complicated. But I am sure Anjali will put smileys wherever she wants in her world.

My way of adding happy energy to my world is to make myself less happy and less energetic and hope that my self-inflicted misery would make others more energetic and happy. Then, wonder why I am not happy anymore while all others

are. Can I stop second-guessing others' reactions to conform to their expectations?

A Return Gift for You: What you give, you get back. You could smile and be happy for no reason without worrying about others' reactions. By being your best self, you can influence the world in a deeper way. You will draw similar people to you. Smile and the world smiles at you.

38
A Thoughtful Gift on Friendship-Day

Friendship Day was near. Anjali made a long list of people she wanted to tie friendship bands to. She bought two packs of bands according to their favourite colours. She then called her friends, visited them and tied bands on their wrists. Everyone was happy. I was amused and touched by the effort she made to get the right bands, call, visit and tie the bands. Good to have a friend like her I thought. As she ran about with her bands I realized that I had not seen a happier soul in a long time.

To my surprise, I received a band too. I thanked her and gave her a big hug. Then she wanted to go to her friend Harsh's house to tie him a band. I dropped her and came home. That's when I saw what was on my table – a gift for me with a little note.

Not only did she think of giving me a band but there was a thoughtful gift for me as well. A pen, for someone who likes to call himself a writer. I wondered why I had not thought of giving her a friendship band? The little note and the glittering pen brought a tear to my eye. When will I learn to give spontaneously? When will I really think of the other person?

Late that night before she went to sleep, I told Anjali how much I loved her gift.

"Where did you get that pen?" I asked.

"I have two pens like that," she said. "So I thought I'll give you one." Then she added. "I thought you may think it's an ordinary pen and lose it among all your other pens so I wrote the note and kept it on your table. There is some glitter in the pen," she explained shyly. I nodded.

"It will look very nice when you write with it. It will be very different from your other pens."

So it will, young one. So it will. You added some glitter in my life as well. Every moment is an opportunity to give. Give. Give. And give.

My way of celebrating friendship is to take my friends for granted, do nothing to make them feel special or wanted, but expect them to understand my sentiments. Then, wonder why my friends are dwindling away slowly. Can I truly celebrate my friendships without holding back?

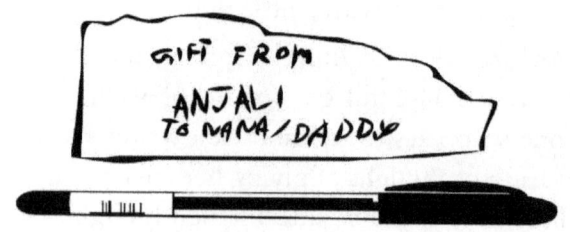

A Return Gift for You: You could honour your friendships from a space of love and gratitude. You could take your friendships beyond a transactional level and create deep, lasting bonds.

Interview with a Four-and-a-Half-Year-Old

It was time I interviewed Anjali again to know what she was thinking about the world. So with her permission, we got down to it one afternoon. Most of the time she was running around the sofa where I sat, pausing only to gather her thoughts or to make a forceful point.

Q. What do you like most?

A. Food. Chicken. Not spicy chicken. Games – Princess games, Dressing up games, King and Queen games, Snow White games, Butterfly games, Karate games and kung fu games.

Q. What do you like doing most?

A. Play games on the computer, Mansi's iPad (a gentle hint to me to buy her one), iPhone (another one) and tennis on Wii Sports.

Q. Who do you like most?

A. Mummy and Daddy. *Attha*s (aunts) – Mythily *attha*. The other *attha*s don't play with me. They give me toys and go off. Mythily *attha* plays with me and asks Ram Bharose (her cook) to cook. I like to feed ants. Take some sugar and sprinkle. Then the ants come running and eat. I like to feed ants. I like to have a pet. Then I can play with it the whole day. A dog. A baby dog (another suggestion for me). But I need Mommy and Daddy dogs too. Or a hamster. They are so cute. Or fishes (worst case scenario).

Q. What do you like at school? (change topic quick)
A. I like the sandpit. Me and Mansi dig there and make a sandcastle. We make sandcastles.

Q. What do you not like?
A. I do not like when *Mamma* shouts at me (sad face). Or when my balloon flies away. I don't like it when they don't have chicken noodles in hotels. I like it with sauce.
I like to take a red leaf or any leaf and paint it the same colour. I like to do that. Not green colour.

Q. What do you think of adults?
A. I think they are nice. I like them. Because they help me.

Q. What makes you happy?
A. When I wear my shiny silver necklaces. I like Chota Bheem movies.

Q. Do you like being happy or unhappy?
A. Happy.

Q. What is happy?
A. Your face goes smiley.

Q. Why happy? Why not unhappy?
A. Shouting, shouting. Crying, crying.

Q. How can we be happy?
A. Think of nice things. Suppose you like sausages. You think of it. You get it. Then you are happy.

That simple huh! But after this, Anjali got tired of the interview and excused herself. Or rather, she ran away to the other room shouting to me that I was asking too many questions and she was getting bored.

Thanks for the interview Anjali. It was very enlightening.

PART 3

HOW TO DEAL WITH PEOPLE

39
My Team Has To Play

We were playing a board game, Anjali and I.

Anjali and her team, Ms. Lamb and Mr. Teddy, celebrating

I played first and then she did. When I reached out to play again she screamed.

"*Nanna*, it is not your turn." She gave me an accusing look, "It is Teddy's turn, *Nanna*."

That was when I noticed that Mr. Teddy and Ms. Lamby, two of her stuffed animals, were seated at the table, with their boards before them.

"They are also playing," she informed me. "What will they do otherwise?"

"But they can't move their pieces Anjali," I told her. "How will they play?"

"It is okay *Nanna*," she told me. "I will play for them."

She proceeded to give both one piece each from the bag, much to the delight of Mr. Teddy and Ms. Lamby, I was sure. They looked quite happy at being allowed to play.

"Okay Teddy," Anjali said, adjusting Teddy. "I will play for you and Lamby okay?"

She smiled at them to indicate that all was well. The rules were tweaked to give Mr. Teddy and Ms. Lamby some advantages so they wouldn't feel bad. As the game progressed, we reached a stage when we were busy helping one another and it did not matter who won!

It was a good lesson in teamwork. To carry everyone along with you, especially those who feel insecure about their place in the team, to make them feel they belong, treat them as equals and support them unconditionally. The best teams support one another and stand up for their friends.

My way of building teams is to judge my team members, exclude and reject most of them because of my biases, and consequently, play with half the strength. Then, wonder why the team is not playing to its full potential. Can I see the unique strengths and possibilities that each member brings to the team?

A Return Gift for You: Bring out the best in your team by accepting everyone as they are, with their unique talents and methods. Allow them to fully express in their own way. Do not impose your way or choose one way over another. They will surprise you.

40
Welcome To Life At My Level

I decided to experience life literally at Anjali's level i.e. three feet from the ground, where she could meet us as equals. I sat on the floor to have lunch and so did Shobha. Anjali was excited with the idea. Since we were down in her world, she automatically became the host. She wanted to serve us and insisted that we eat this or have another helping of that. It was almost like we were visiting her in her home. She took charge, as if she were saying "I know you guys are not used to this so let me help you out."

Watching Anjali's growing excitement, involvement and infectious enthusiasm, I realized that by adding just a wee bit of imagination to our daily tasks, we could make work interesting. Doing things differently energizes everyone, makes make them want to join the party and contribute. All we had done in this case was sit on the floor.

It was also interesting to notice how Anjali assumed ownership and became the host. The moment she felt that she was dealing with us from her own space, she automatically became the boss. She felt secure, opened up and took ownership intuitively.

My way of making others take ownership for their role is to tell them to own their jobs, but force my ideas on them, and control their space. Then, wonder why they do not take more ownership and why I end up doing everything. Can I be secure enough to let my team members own their space, and do things their way?

A Return Gift for You: You could achieve more by doing less. Allow your team members space, step back and let them contribute. Get out of the way.

41
Give Only When Asked

Anjali and I were in the car when we stopped at a traffic signal. An old lady was begging for alms and came towards us.

I had some candy in the car dashboard and decided to give it to her.

Anjali warned, "Give it only when she asks."

"Why?" I asked.

"What if she does not want it? You see, if a cat does not want to drink milk, it might push it away right? Even the old lady might not like it if you give without asking."

I could not agree more. Why did I assume that the old lady would want candy just because I had some? How could I have been so caught up in my image of a generous giver?

My way of 'giving' is to feel superior because I am in a position to 'give' — gracelessly and thoughtlessly. Even while receiving, I twist things so I feel like I am actually 'giving' to the other person by 'taking' from them. Then, wonder why the world does not recognize my generosity. Can I give with the attitude of 'having already received'?

A Return Gift for You: When you give, give from a space of gratitude and not with arrogance. Be aware that you are the beneficiary in the act. Be grateful that someone is giving you an opportunity to give by receiving from you.

42
Is Hugging Boys Bad?

We had finally arrived at the subject of gender issues.

"You know, I was very upset today," said Anjali as she hopped into the car after school.

"Why?" I asked.

"I went to class in the morning and met Harsh. We hugged each other. We normally do. And then Gowri came and asked why I hugged him. I said I hugged him because we were friends. What's wrong with that?"

The entire tirade was delivered in one agitated breath. But Anjali was not done.

"I told Gowri that hugs were good. She said hugging girls is okay but not boys. So I said Harsh is my friend. So what if he is a boy?. And then Harsh came and said that I hugged him first which was not true. I told him that he hugged me first and I put my arms around him. Then Harsh accepted and said that he hugged me first."

She was even more upset by now.

Then when our teacher came, she saw that I was upset. I asked her if hugging our friends was wrong. She said it was not and that I shouldn't be sad for such small things. Then she took Gowri aside and told her something.

"So what if he is a boy *Nanna*? Why do we have to treat them differently? What if someone's skin colour is different? Should we treat them differently?"

"No," I said. "In fact hugging is good. Give me one."

Is there a right and a wrong in an act of friendship? Of love? How often do I sit in judgement and perpetrate confusion?

My way of dealing with sensitive gender issues is to label, discriminate, and separate - because I am incapable of handling such fine emotions myself. Then, wonder why it's all so complex. Can I be aware that my strong reactions to finer human emotions comes from a space of fear and insecurity?

A Return Gift for You: You could enjoy the beauty and joy in an act of love or friendship. Don't feel threatened by it. Be open and receptive to finer emotions. True strength comes from being vulnerable. True power comes from love.

43
Adding to the Green Day Pot

It is Environment Day at Daksha School. The children were to dress in green. Anjali wore her green dress. She was excited about participating in the debate on the use of plastic. "I chose to speak on 'No to plastic'," she said.

Minutes before we left for school I saw her doing something hurriedly. A closer look revealed that she had cut up some papers, pulled out her crayons and paints and was working with great focus. I wondered what the last minute activity was about but decided to wait outside in the car. Shortly, Anjali climbed in too.

"See *Nanna*," she said. "A green hair pin." She had cut out a small paper flower, painted it green and stuck it onto her hair pin. All to go with the environment theme. Nice!

"How did you do that?" I asked.

"I was wearing the green dress and thought I could do something more. I cut out the paper flower but it did not come out right. So I drew the flower again and made *Mamma* cut it. Then I painted it green but it did not look so good. So I coloured it with a crayon and then had *Mamma* stick it on the pin. Do you like it?"

Wow! That was a lot of work for a hair pin. "It looks great," I said.

It's a comment on the environment at her school too – on teachers who encourage participation. Creating a nurturing, learning and interactive space for children is probably the greatest change in environment we can bring about in this world. Well done, Daksha School and Anita, the tireless, caring Principal and the guiding light of Anjali's wonderful school.

My way of participating in a cause is to sign up to participate quickly so I get participation certificates and any freebies, be reluctant with my contribution and give only as much as required. Then, wonder why my contribution isn't getting the appreciation it should. Can I get over my What's-In-It-For-Me attitude and contribute in every way to help my team?

A Return Gift for You: By contributing your best to the team effort you grow; you do not lose. Add to the team effort wholeheartedly wherever you are, whatever team you are a part of. It keeps you alive and growing. When you hold back, you shrink.

44
Good Teachers and Bad Teachers

Anjali and I were discussing the teachers she liked. And also the ones she didn't fancy so much.

Turns out the teachers she liked were funny, kind, interesting and a little strict (not too strict, but she imitated how they would go about the class with a little frown on her face)

The teachers she does not like are either too angry, punish students and do not understand them or are *boring*! She also did not like the ones who stick to a certain way of doing things even when she cannot follow their way. For example, she told me her music sir kept trying to make her change the 1,2,3 and 4 even when she could not follow it and she lost interest in his class.

The formula then, for a good teacher, from a seven-year-old's perspective, seemed to be fun, interesting, kind, compassionate, patient, a bit strict, not short tempered and certainly, not unjust. I guess 'interesting' makes learning an engaging experience while 'kind', 'compassionate' and 'just' create a trusting atmosphere.

'So do you like teachers who are strict or the ones who are not strict?' I persisted.

After some thought, she responded. "I like teachers who are kind," she said.

Kindness, it appears, is important to children. The more I think of it, the more I am convinced that kindness is the quality one should cultivate.

My concept of teaching is to tell and not listen, demonstrate and not allow the student to experience, and not bother much about making things interesting – after all it's their job to learn. Then, wonder why my students are not performing well despite all my hard work. Can I focus on teaching effectively instead of showing off what I know?

A Return Gift for You: Judge yourself as a teacher not by how much you know, but by how well you impart what you know. Allow students to question, find solutions and enjoy the joy of learning. True learning happens when you open up possibilities and let the students discover. Ignite the spark and step out of the way.

45
We Don't Know if They Are Happy

I asked Anjali.

"Was *Mamma* happy when she saw you off to school today?"

(I knew *Mamma* had been a bit hassled, hence the question.)

Anjali thought for a moment.

"She looked happy," she said slowly.

Then she thought some more.

"But we don't know," she explained. "Sometimes people appear to be something on the outside and but are something else on the inside."

I looked at her.

"Can you sense that?" I asked.

"Yes," she said. "I can make out when they are not fully happy inside but they are smiling outside."

We think people can't see the truth, but people see through us. People can make out when there is a gap between our thoughts and acts, our feelings and our behaviour. People can sense that something is not right.

My way of expressing and communicating my feelings to others who support me is to feel one thing, say something remove and do something else. Then, wonder why the people who are closest to me don't understand me at all. Can I be authentic?

A Return Gift for You: To be understood by others you need to understand yourself first. Align your thoughts, feelings and actions. Then you will first understand yourself – and be understood by others.

46
My Friends Are Different Parts of Me

"She won – again," said Anjali, distressed that Mansi had beaten her at chess once more.

After a little discussion and advice on the technicalities of the game, I gently told Anjali to go back and play another game.

"No, Mansi does not want to play chess again," she pouted.

"Why?" I asked.

"She does not like playing chess so much. Harsh likes playing chess. They like doing different things."

After a moment she said, "they are like different parts of me. Mansi is like the active part. She likes dancing, jumping and colouring. Harsh is the non-active part. He likes playing chess and other games."

Hmm.

It took me a long time to figure that out. How two of my closest friends could be so different. Some of them hate each other but resonate with different parts of me perfectly, albeit, separately.

I have a tiny bit of all of my friends in me. I am a bit of everything really. The best and the worst.

My way of viewing myself in relation to the world is to first fix an image of myself (in glowing terms normally) and reject all other possibilities as alien to me. Then, wonder why other aspects that I have rejected are showing up around me, within me and irritating me. Can I accept that every person I know resonates with some part within me, and is an unalienable part of me?

A Return Gift for You: You could see that everyone in your life complements different parts of you – the good and the bad. When you accept that you are all of them and they are all of you, life is easier to deal with.

47
If You Can't Appreciate, Shut Up!

Anjali drew a cartoon strip, complete with drawings and dialogue, inspired by the *Suppandi* jokes in the *Tinkle* Digest. It was well illustrated, had a clear structure and looked as good as any professional job, (even more so) for a seven-year-old.

My first reaction was praise for her effort. Suppandi looked perfect and the joke was well made.

But then the adult in me took over. "You know… you could have had that guy say this… and this guy say that… and it could have been funnier," I said.

She looked at me, disappointed. "It's my cartoon. I'll do it this way only."

This is a classic example of how we demotivate children with our thoughtless responses.

Anjali had conceived the entire idea in a particular way and executed it all by herself, and quite well at that. Instead of appreciating her creativity and initiative, I took all the fun out of it with my unnecessary comments. Whatever she did was a source of pride to her. Why did I have to spoil it? Why did I have this need to correct everything? Why didn't I shut up?

Criticism kills the spirit. With such insensitive reactions, children just give up on creating things. In my quest to create perfection in others' lives (and not my own of course) I take my criticism to work, family, friends and kill that joyful spirit in people. So, could I shut up with my criticism NOW.

To motivate, they say, don't seek perfection – seek progress. Focus on what is being done right, however little. We are all work in progress. Nobody's perfect. I can't do that cartoon half as well as Anjali had. So could I appreciate the good work please?

My way of handling the role of a mentor or a coach is to be critical of errors, pass unnecessary judgments and give advice that makes the ward feel small (and myself big). Then, wonder why the ward is losing interest in spite of my best efforts. Can I be more tolerant, patient and appreciative of others? And with myself?

A Return Gift for You: To facilitate better work from your team, acknowledge the effort and appreciate what they did right. When they know they have your support they will produce even better work. Be gentle. Don't push them down, if you want them to rise high.

48. I Can Support Your Opponent For You

Anjali and I were playing a game of table tennis on the Wii. I was playing and had secured a decent lead of 4-1 (a game finishes at 6 points). When I conceded a point carelessly, Anjali cautioned me – "Finish the game *Nanna*. If you lose more points, the other fellow will win."

I lost another point. Now the game was getting tight.

"I will cheer both of you," she decided suddenly. "I will cheer whoever wins a point."

I was surprised. Why was she cheering the other player? I made up my mind not to concede any more points. I played hard and soon won the game.

She was happy.

"I know a technique to make you play better," she said.

"What technique?" I asked.

"When I cheer the other player you will get angry *na*, and then you will play even better? That way you will win."

Wow.

"Where did you learn the technique?" I asked.

"Mansi taught me this," she said. "The other day, Mansi's brother Kushal and I were playing a game when

Mansi started cheering him loudly. I asked her why she was cheering him and not me, Mansi said – If I cheer him you will get angry and play well and beat him. That's where I learned this technique."

Some serious motivational technique. Challenging a person's ability is probably one of the most effective ways to motivate him to give his best. If the intent, while challenging the ability is to bring out the best in the other person, it motivates. If the intent is about proving that you know more, you could demotivate the person. It's a thin line. But if you love your friends, you'd probably do it even at the risk of becoming unpopular.

My method of motivating my friends to better their performances is to superficially encourage them with words that mean nothing because any unpleasant feedback might offend them. Then, wonder why my friends do not trust my advice nor want me in their corner. Can I find the courage and love to do what's good for my friends and what helps them even if it is unpleasant?

A Return Gift for You: You could genuinely help your friend turn in a better performance and grow, even at the cost of being unpopular with him for a while. That's what friends are for. A moment of unpleasantness is better for him than a lifetime of being nice and stuck. Be honest to your role and to your friend.

The Unforgettable Fruit Day Incident

Anjali's school has a 'Fruit Day' every week. One child is nominated to bring a fruit of his/her choice on this day. The fruits are then cut and shared in class. It's fun and challenging and the kids love the exercise – the cutting of fruits, the sharing, the planning, the responsibility etc. It's a deviously simple idea to involve children in so many important aspects of life. It's just what an 'interesting' teacher would do.

Anjali got her chance. She was super excited. But she did not make a note in her diary and forgot. It was soon somebody else's turn. She was quite penitent and asked her teacher for another chance. However, her teacher told her that she had had her opportunity and that she should wait till it was her turn again.

Anjali was pretty upset about it. It became a matter of trust with her. She was teary eyed when she narrated how she asked teacher everyday if she could bring the fruit but was told to wait for her turn. At home emotions rose. *How? What?* Maybe we should talk to the teacher and so on. The drama continued for a week but there was nothing we could do. It seemed deadlocked.

Next week Anjali came home and announced, "Tomorrow is Fruit Day. It's my chance." She instructed me to get five of the best pomegranates in the market.

How did this happen? Anjali told us how.

"I went to my teacher and said please auntie, please auntie, I will not forget this time auntie, I will write down now only in the diary auntie, I won't forget again auntie, please auntie give me one chance... please auntie, please auntie..." and on and on until her teacher gave in.

That's how Anjali got the job. The seemingly tragic story got a happy twist thanks to an act of ownership. And a creative intervention.

How can you stop someone who is so earnest? Most times it is what gets the job done. Sensing that all other routes (save parental interference) were closed and that she still wanted to participate badly, Anjali decided that her best hope was to put her ego aside and plead. It was between her and her teacher. If you show how badly you want something, that you are prepared to die for it, you'll get it. She did it of her own volition which is what makes it interesting. Good job Anjali. Now I only hope the pomegranates I bought measure up to your effort.

My way of handling a roadblock is to withdraw at the first sign of resistance, plead my case half-heartedly, resent the authority concerned for not understanding my position and give up on what I want without fully expressing myself. Then, wonder why I never get what I want. Can I persist and fully express myself until others understand what I want and how badly I want it?

A Return Gift for You: To get what you want set your ego aside. When you approach your goal with no ego, you commit fully and give it everything you have. When you're stuck, look for where your ego is coming in the way.

50
A Surprise Gift For Harsh

Even before we left Bangalore, Anjali was preparing for her friend Harsh's birthday. Harsh was not expecting her to return in time for his birthday so Anjali planned to surprise him by dropping in on his birthday party. She crafted a birthday card in advance with colourful designs and stickers and hid it away.

She had not decided on a gift though. While shopping in Bangalore with her Mom, Anjali saw a cricket bat and gloves and wanted to gift them to Harsh. Shobha called me and asked if she should buy them. I told her that Anjali would get more choice in a sports shop. Could she wait another day?

Anjali postponed her purchase. There's something about delaying gratification in such decisions, because it's not easy. It comes from a deep space of love to want the best for someone you care about.

When we reached Hyderabad the next day we stopped at the Decathlon store near the Shamshabad airport. I found a good bat for Anjali and she took it happily, taking a stance and checking if it was comfortable. She picked a tennis ball to go with it.

I asked her why she thought of buying Harsh a bat.

"You know how crazy he is about cricket," she said. "He is always playing inside his house. He has a ball strung from the ceiling and practices with it. The other day I saw that the rubber on his bat was torn. I thought he might like a new bat." Ah, how I wish I had friends like Anjali when I was playing with broken bats and torn grips.

When we went home she wanted to gift-wrap it. I could not imagine how anyone could wrap a cricket bat and ball. But what she did with packing that bat and ball in gold and blue foil took my breath away. Harsh was a lucky fellow.

And then we were off to his house. We arrived earlier than the other guests. Harsh Fozdar who was not expecting Anjali for his party was in for a huge surprise as Anjali walked in to his house, and with a rather odd shaped gift in her hand. I wasn't there to capture the moment but it must have been nice. Later, I asked Anjali how he reacted.

"He does not show anything on his face," she shrugged. "Just normal."

I told Anjali that I wished I had friends like her. She smiled.

"I am friends with you too na *Nanna*," she reassured me. That's comforting to know. I'd like to have friends like her any day. Now where is that old bat of mine with the torn grip?

My way of giving gifts is to show up (big gift!), present a token gift and keep an eye open for the goodies I might be getting in return. Then, wonder why there is no give and take in my relationships. Can I give wholeheartedly without expecting anything from the other?

A Return Gift for You: Your gift shows the thoughtfulness, respect and love you bring to the relationship. When you give gifts as a ritual, the lack of thought and love shows. Spend time thinking, not reaching for your wallet.

51
A Lesson in Energy Management

"Maybe I should not have gotten so angry," I told Anjali. We were on our way to school after a needless argument I had with Shobha. Anjali nodded in agreement.

"That's what I do," she said gently.

"Do what?" I enquired.

"When someone shouts at me, even I feel like shouting. But what's the use? The roof will break with all that shouting," she said.

"So what do you do?" I asked.

"I go lower," she said, using her hands to show how she steps down the energy. "We should go lower, so the other person also goes lower, then you go more lower, and then the other person also will, and it will soon be over."

"What happens if we don't?" I asked.

"Then it goes higher," she said, showing the steps in which arguments rise. "It will go higher and higher and higher and hit the roof."

I nodded. I could use this. Like they say, do you want to be right or do you want to be happy.

It's the best class in energy management I have had. Now all I had to do was to remember the visual of Anjali's small hands going lower, step by step.

My way of handling an unpleasant situation is to allow the situation to develop needlessly, react angrily, fuel-rising tempers, get mad with the other person for not seeing that I am right and hold the other person responsible for the flare up. Then, wonder how these situations get so out of control despite my best efforts. Can I stop taking things personally?

A Return Gift for You: You have the power to defuse any situation from escalating into something unpleasant by stepping back, not forcing your views and seeing things from the other person's perspective. When you let go of your ego, you could change the outcome drastically. Step back to go forward.

52
A Master Class in Coaching

The toy Spiderman flies in the air if you pull a string. If you do it right, he flies nice and high. Otherwise he does not take off.

Anjali was teaching her aunt Mythily *attha* how to launch Spiderman. Her aunt pulled the string gently and Spiderman did not fly. He refused to even eject from the base. Now what? It was a classic coaching situation. Anjali's ward was not performing. Was it a skill or a will issue? What would Anjali do?

Anjali addressed the skill issue first.

"Hold the base in this direction," she said. "Then it will happen."

Anjali did not do it herself but made her *attha* do it.

The skill aspect addressed, she urged her *attha* to try again. This time Spiderman flew, but fell short of expectations. Now what? Do we give up?

Anjali did neither. She was patient. She smiled and put her aunt at ease. She gave her *attha* a smaller, clearer target.

"Do it again," she said. "Now try to touch this line. Okay?"

With a clear and achievable target, a supportive coach and some training, her *attha* fared much better this time. Spiderman flew effortlessly to the new target.

A round of instant and genuine appreciation followed from the young coach.

"Very good," said Anjali fetching the toy in obvious delight. Then she increased the distance of the target. 'This time make Superman fly till the door.'

Knowing that she was on the right track and that she could rely on her coach's guidance, Anjali's *attha* tried again. Spiderman took off, flew confidently, and hit the door. Goal achieved. There were high-fives all round.

It was a fine lesson in coaching. Address skill issues, set achievable targets, make the ward feel secure by being supportive, encourage progress and revise target each time. Anjali corrected her *attha's* technique, did not get upset when she failed, redirected her energies and encouraged her. Once her *attha* figured out the way to do things and gained confidence, she did not have to bother her again. Good coaching.

My way of handling team members who are not delivering is to give them a stiff target, wait for them to fail, show my displeasure and set them up for more failure. Then, wonder why I get stuck with poor talent. Can I judge my coaching capability on the basis of my team's performances?

A Return Gift for You: You could take all your relationships to the next level if you approached them from a coaching perspective. Don't waste your time proving how right you are; get the job done by them so they learn and grow.

53

The 2 Ways to Get Things Done

I was complaining about someone not doing their job when I heard Anjali.

"*Nanna*, there are two types of people."

"What types?" I asked.

"For the first type, you have to shout and scold and only then will they work. With the second, all you have to do is be kind, and they will work."

I was impressed. It took me a long time to understand that everyone responds differently and that there is no one magic formula to deal with everyone.

"Okay. I know the first sort," I said. "They take advantage of our patient, trusting and kind nature and do not do any work. So you have to shout at them. But what about the second type? How can I get them to work?"

She seemed to know this — mostly from experience I guess.

"You must make them feel comfortable," she said, "with kind words. Then they will understand and do the work. If you shout at them they will not work."

She seemed to have pretty firm views about that. I had a feeling that it had something to do with her experiences with me. So I decided to get some feedback.

"Some shout and some listen. What type am I?"

Silence.

Surprising, because I thought the answer was easy. I am the kind and listening type!

I prodded more gently.

"Say out of 10 times, do I shout more times or listen more times?"

"50-50," was the answer.

Hmmm. Needs work.

My way of getting people to perform is to use one method to fit all — which is MY method — they can fall in line or fail. Then, wonder why the team is failing to perform. Can I find ways to enable the best performances from each of my wards?

A Return Gift for You: To bring the best out of each member of your team, invest time and find the key that motivates them to do their best. Everyone has a different key, and once you find it, you can facilitate great work. There are no shortcuts.

54
Could We Be More Polite Please?

We had enlisted the support of Niveditha, Anjali's painting teacher (and friend) to help with Anjali's school project. I was ticking off things that the project work needed.

"Okay," I told Anjali at the end. "Let's tell aunty that we have all these items. We can ask her what else she wants."

Anjali was pensive.

"What?" I asked.

She pointed out gently.

"Maybe we could say 'what else do we need?' instead of asking her 'what else do you want?'" She said, "It would be more kind and polite. It is our work after all."

I got the subtle difference.

"Yes indeed," I agreed and handed her my phone. "Could you send her a message please?"

She typed a polite message that was in line with her intentions.

I wonder how much I take others for granted, and how it reflects in my words and actions. I must thank you Anjali for making me more aware.

My way of asking for help is to ask for help, dump the entire job on the person who offered to help me, behave as if it's their responsibility now and be unhappy with them for not doing it right. Then, wonder how unhelpful the world is. Can I be less self-centred and more sensitive to others?

A Return Gift for You: To get more support from the environment treat it gently and sensitively. Choose your words and actions carefully and do not take things for granted. No one owes you anything.

55
They Copy Actions, Not Words

Shobha and I were discussing role models and how children imitate the actions of their teachers. Anjali, who was playing nearby, overheard us and piped in.

"Our teacher always tells us not to talk when we are eating. But she always talks to a*kka* when she is having her lunch. It's not fair. How is it that she can do it but we cannot?"

"Maybe," I tried. "She is discussing important things with a*kka*?"

"No," said Anjali emphatically, "she is not discussing important things. We can hear her. She discusses normal things just like we do."

Ah. We changed the topic.

A few days later, we were going to drop Anjali at school.

"Anjali, I forgot to do my hair," said Shobha to Anjali. "I told you to do yours but forgot to do mine."

Pat came the reply.

"That's why you must do it first before you tell others."

I wonder how many times authority figures say one thing and do another. How many times injustice is perceived by those who suffer it and how rarely they get a chance to voice it?

Children follow our actions, not our words. Their behaviour reflects our actions.

My approach to being a role model is to say the right thing but do something else and expect people to follow my words and not my actions. Then, wonder why they are not getting it despite my telling them so many times. Can I align my thoughts, words and my behaviours?

A Return Gift for You: You could change the world not just by words but by actions that back your words. Any change you desire in the world comes when you change yourself. You make a bigger impact by doing and being the change you want to see.

Interview with a Five-Year-Old

Cool huh. Though there's more black than grey.

Courtesy – Sagar

Q. What do you like doing?
A. Playing with my friends. Jumping. Even if I get hurt I like playing. Dancing, painting... I like ballet dancing.

Q. What are the things you don't like?
A. Eating vegetables, getting scolded by *Mamma* and making Mansi upset. Sometimes we make each other upset.

Q. What are the things you like to eat?
A. Ice cream, vanilla, cakes, strawberry and chocolates.

Q. What do you like to play with Mansi?
A. Treasure hunt, Ice water, Hide and Seek, School-School, Mummy-Daddy, bowling, cricket and football.

Q. What books do you like?
A. A Mad, Mad, Mad World; Blue's Clues, Pepper, Panchatantra, Aesop's fables, Enid Blyton's books.

Q. What cartoons do you like?
A. Ninja Hattori, Doraemon, I am telling the shows, not the characters I like okay? Chota Bheem, and I like Chutki in Chota Bheem.

Q. Movies?
A. Chashme Baddoor, Lion King, Stuart Little... I like those the most.

Q. Why?
A. I like them, that's all.

Q. Do you like crying or laughing?
A. Laughing... because I am a laugher.

Q. What are the things you'd like to have?
A. Good pants because all my pants and jeans have holes in them and... and... what else... I would like to have an alarm clock too I think.

Q. Why?
A. Because these days school starts early, so if I have an alarm clock I can get up early

Q. What do you like about school?
A. I like studying. Knowledge. Math. Teachers, friends, classmates... I like Mansi.

Q. Why do you like knowledge?
(She got agitated a bit at this seemingly stupid question.)
A. Because if there was no knowledge on earth I would not know anything. But because of knowledge I can grow, learn, talk, how to end sentences, what I don't know. I don't know somethings. I don't know science. I need to know science. I need knowledge to be a scientist, an architect... see you can't write books without knowledge. You can't do anything without knowledge. I love knowledge.

I decided to veer off this topic.

Q. What do you think of *Nanna*?
A. He's so tall, like a giant. He always likes to write. He always makes me write in my new books, always buys me whatever I want. Always he does the same thing, again and again, everyday he spills my medicines, everyday he keeps looking at the computer. I don't understand why he goes to the computer.

Q. What about *Mamma*?
A. I don't have words. She's everything. She's like a lion to me. Everyday she goes rushing about the house doing everything and more.

Q. What do you think about yourself?
A. I like my body, myself, my brains, my thoughts, my feelings and my toys and things... this is what I like about myself.

Q. Who else do you like?
A. Teachers, parents and God.

Q. Who is God?
A. You don't know God?

Q. I never saw Him.
A. You can't see Him. You can feel Him.

Q. Can you feel Him?
A. I can feel Him. He's inside my brain. I can feel.

Q. How does it feel?
A. First tell me who made me. God. Who gave my nose? Mansi? Heart? Parents? See everything God only. Who gave me water? See everything God has given me.

Q. God is good?
A. Yes. Now you understand why He is inside me. He came inside me just to help me.

Q. Will He be inside me?
A. Yes *Nanna*. God is inside everybody. My favourite God is Ganesha.

Q. If you want to ask God for one thing what would you ask?
A. I'll ask God to help me in my studies, in my races, in my tough games. I used to ask God only for toys but now I ask for courage.

Q. Why?
A. Courage can help me do anything.

Q. How?
A. Courage is my partner. Whenever I have some difficulty, only courage is my partner. Courage will help me in everything.

Q. What about money? What do you think about it?
A. It helps us live. If we do not have money we cannot eat. How can we buy from Ratnadeep (our super market)? We always need lots of money.

Q. How can we get money?
A. If we work.

Q. What is the happiest thing you remember?
A. Mansi.

Q. Do you like interviews?
A. Yes, I like interviews.

Q. Do you want to add anything?
A. My favourite stories are 3 Billy Goats Gruff, Cinderella and Rapunzel,

Q. One more question. Who makes you laugh?
A. Choudary *mama*, Mythily *attha*, Ranjan *mama*, *Mamma*...sometimes I only makes jokes and laugh.

Thus ended the interview. I was impressed with her take on God, courage and knowledge. There's always something new to learn when I interview her.

Thanks Anjali. For some more illuminating perspectives.

PART 4

HOW TO APPROACH LIFE

It's Not the Size Dummy; It's the Learning

We visited a friend who had a regular-sized table tennis table. After the grownups finished playing, three-year-old Anjali wanted to play too. Not just hit the ball, but she actually played with an adult across the table. For someone who was just about the height of the table, she hit a few balls. I wondered what makes children do such heroic stuff.

Another instance was with the exercise bike at home. Anjali was fascinated by it and would sit on it while I pedalled. It's a hard machine for a three-year-old to operate but she tried everyday and pushed at the pedal with all her might, with no success. One day I heard the beep that the machine makes when someone starts it. Anjali had somehow climbed on it and put in enough effort to move the pedals – backwards – but she moved them. Nothing is too big for her it appears.

For someone of her size, everything must appear complex and difficult. But she sees no limitations and takes on things much bigger than her size and capability, and by sheer desire and perseverance, succeeds.

Perhaps it helps not to know words like difficulty, failure and fear. What seems to come naturally to her is learning – and fast. The more I discourage her from doing things, the more she wants to try them, even crying and making a scene till I give in. On the other hand I see adults who freeze at the thought of learning anything new. How does our education system turn natural learners into such defensive and insecure personalities?

So a three-year-old Anjali places her hand over mine when I was changing gears in the car and asks "Which gear *Nanna?*" She wants to open the house lock despite the lack of light in the porch and searches endlessly for the keyhole – without giving up. She climbs the biggest slide in the park and slides down at terrifying speeds. She wants to play with her older cousins at games where she is no match for them and tries her best to defeat them. She takes every new toy and figures how to operate it. She sits for long hours trying to puzzle over everything until it makes some sense. She does this again and again. She wants to help me with gardening. She wants to handle the computer mouse when her rhymes are playing on YouTube. She wants to make calls on the mobile to her *Ajji*. She wants click the camera herself. She wants to use the fork and spoon at the dining table and chopsticks at the Chinese restaurant. She wants to pay the chap who comes to collect the newspaper bill. She wants to spot the moon first. She wants to answer the bell each time it rings. She does dangerous things like running full tilt on all sorts of hard and uneven surfaces without a sense of balance, jumping on the sofa as if it were a trampoline, wanting to pat an unfriendly dog on the street or walking into pouring rain with an umbrella.

This quality of hers – to fearlessly try anything new, to learn at any cost, to rise to every challenge however unfamiliar or tough, is a quality that could transform life from mundane to electric.

Me? My patterns are set. I go to the same places. Same seats, same people, same games. My world is stagnant, in the known space, and as a result, limited. I must have been like Anjali when I was her age. What happened to me?

My way of looking at the many learning opportunities I come across everyday is to avoid them, view them as unnecessary obstacles, complain about how they hinder my progress, sidestep the learning and repeat the process. Then, wonder why my life is not moving forward in spite of avoiding all the obstacles in my way. Can I regain that spirit and the excitement of learning that I had when I was three years old?

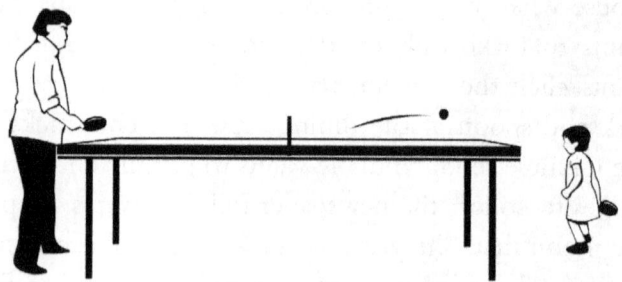

A Return Gift for You: You can learn much faster if you look forward to meeting the obstacles in your life as learning opportunities. Each time you say 'yes' to an obstacle you learn some more. Dive headlong into new challenges everyday.

57 Learning Quickly Through Imitation

These days Anjali imitates whatever she sees or hears. From expressions on people's faces to those on animation pictures, nursery rhymes and songs, she imitates things all the time. Baloo, the bear says something in 'The Jungle Book' and she repeats it. There's a new rhyme at school, and she sings it all day. She asks me to play *'Lakdi ki kathi…'* on the car stereo so she can sing along.

Even though she gets it wrong most times, she is not afraid to imitate, fail, and be corrected. She repeats the corrected version immediately without skipping a beat and off she goes, new and improved. There is no ego involved. Of course there are times when she insists that she has got it right and we have it all wrong, and there is nothing one can do about that. But those times are rare.

It's the non-attachment to 'right', that makes her so flexible and such a scene-stealer. She flows freely in tune with nature. Whatever she finds interesting she imitates and learns instantly.

On the other hand I think of my rigid opinions and beliefs. I am right. You are wrong. To protect what I think is right, I fight the world. So rigid are my opinions that I cannot bend and I hold on to them hard even if I have to break. Could one imitate nature, which flows in harmony, and shows one the way?

How To Approach Life

My way of adopting anything new is to be highly suspicious of it, refuse to accept it, find fault with it and decide to learn it on my own even If I have to reinvent the wheel. Then, wonder why I am lagging behind. Can I become childlike when confronted with anything new?

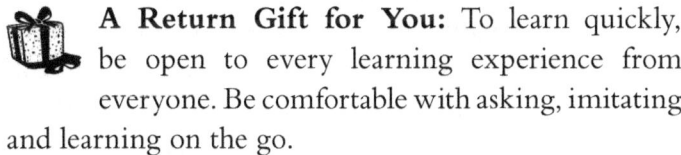 **A Return Gift for You:** To learn quickly, be open to every learning experience from everyone. Be comfortable with asking, imitating and learning on the go.

58
The Great Car Cleaning Project

The car was dirty after a grueling 550-km drive from Hyderabad to Pune. I asked Anjali (who was three at that time) if she would help me clean it. "Come *Nanna*, let us clean the car now," she began enthusiastically. I asked her to wait. I wanted to read the newspaper first. She started crying. "Let us do it now." I told her to fetch a cloth and some water hoping to distract her. She appeared with both in a couple of minutes, one in each hand. I had no escape.

Anjali chose the lower parts of the car to clean. I took the upper parts. Then, there was silence. I wondered if she'd got bored and gone away. I peered around the back of the car to look for her. There she was, scrubbing away. She smiled, "It is so dirty *na Nanna*," she said as she worked on the number plate. After a few strokes she exclaimed gleefully, "see how clean it is now."

I was done. But Anjali was still working on that number plate. "It is still dirty *Nanna*," she said pointing to the stubborn marks. She made more trips to get water, knelt by the car and worked until she was fully satisfied with the result. Then and only then, did she sign off from the job, tired but happy.

I worked in organizations that paid me to work but I don't think I ever worked with such involvement. Anjali couldn't wait to start work, decided by herself what to work at, figured out how to do things on her own, set her own quality standards and gave it everything she had with no expectation of recognition or return. Most importantly, she took pride in her work. Surely a better work ethic than mine.

My approach to work is to start tentatively, look around for appreciation and applause, and withdraw in disappointment when I don't receive recognition for my half-hearted effort. Then, wonder why my capabilities are not recognized and why I am not given an opportunity to display them. Can I disconnect my work from reward and recognition? Can I approach work as if it was an opportunity to leave my mark?

A Return Gift for You: To do great work, take up every job with your mind, body and soul. Do it enthusiastically and wholeheartedly. Your work is your identity.

59 The Knight Is Clever Only If We Are Clever

We were playing chess while Anjali was extolling the virtues of the knight.

"The horse is tricky, very clever no *Nanna*," she said while arranging the pieces on the board. She was still getting a hang of how the knight moves and how it can cause havoc in the game. I agreed sagely.

She thought for a moment and corrected herself.

"But the horse is clever only if we are clever right?"

True. It's not about the resources ever; it's how we use them that matters. We still have to do the work – understand capabilities, limitations and potential and then deploy the resource accordingly to get the best results. It goes for everything. Life, relationships, work and health – we must make them work.

My way of making my knights perform better is to hope that the knight will perform by itself because it has ability and talent, sack it for non-performance if it does not match my high expectations, get another knight to replace it, and repeat procedure. Then, wonder why I am stuck with knights that do not perform. Can I see my team members' failure as my failure?

A Return Gift for You: To get the best out of your team take it upon yourself to find ways that make them perform better. Even if they have ability and talent, it is you who has to make them realize and perform to their potential. Don't sit on your high horse; you will miss great opportunities.

60
Try It First, And Then Decide

What to wear remains a regular dilemma of mine. To help me decide, I ask Anjali sometimes. She seems to be clearer-headed and decisive than I am in this, as in many other matters.

I asked her whether the t-shirt I was wearing was fine or if she thought I should change.

"First show me the others you want to wear," the three-and-a-half-year-old said taking charge of the situation. I showed her. While I was rummaging through the prospective T-shirts she stood behind me – "Look for something that does not poke you, something that is soft." It is a big thing for her that clothes should be comfortable. Made sense. I gave up on one of the more stylish T-shirts and chose a plain white one. She felt it and nodded. Not poky.

I asked if I could now wear the new T-shirt. Pat came the answer. *"Nanna*, first wear it. Only then will you know if it is really not poky and if it is soft. First wear it and then decide."

Ah, if only I had this sense before I bought my many shirts, pants, shoes, socks, ideologies, philosophies and relationships that later grew poky and uncomfortable. Anyway, better late than never. I tried on the white tee. It was better than the one I was wearing. So there I was going out with a T-shirt that may not look as good, but which was very comfortable indeed. And it made me smile a bit more!

What I feel also matters.

My way of choosing comfort for myself is to get uncomfortable with the idea of treating myself well, decide that I do not deserve anything special and pick up the first thing I see because it does not matter anyway. Then, wonder why I am so uncomfortable all the time. Can I put myself first?

A Return Gift for You: To choose for yourself, first accept that you are worthy of the best. Choose with love and care as you would for a special person. You deserve it the most; you're the hero in your life.

61
Why Feel What You Don't Feel

I was talking to Anjali about something and the word 'happiness' cropped up.

"How can one be happy?" I asked.

"Smile," said Anjali simply.

"Oh," I said, "and when we are sad, then how to be happy?"

"*Arre,*" she said, exasperated with all this convoluted talk. "Why do you have to do anything? If you are happy, be happy, if you are sad, be sad. That's all. Why do you need to learn something else?"

This ended that particular conversation.

My way of dealing with my emotions is to imagine unnecessary scenarios, analyze, second guess myself, resist what is and mess it all up for myself in the present. Then, wonder why I am not happy anymore. Can I feel what I am feeling instead of fighting it?

A Return Gift for You: You could enjoy peace and equanimity if you accept the moment as it is and what it brings. When you go deep into the moment, instead of fighting it, it passes sooner than you think. It's dealt with, and not stored for later.

62
Let Us Go Only if It's Important

I have this crazy need to get out of home by four in the evening and go somewhere. I don't know why, but I just can't sit at home. Now, ever since her vacation has begun, Anjali has been noticing this particular habit of mine. I ask her everyday, "shall we go out?" hoping to entice her.

"No," she says. "I want to stay at home only."

Some days I convince her. Some days I can't.

Once, when I asked her again, for the umpteenth time if she wanted to go anywhere, she said,

"No. Let us be at home only."

I decided to fall in step and not force the issue as I normally do.

"No problem," I said, "there is no need to go anywhere. We'll stay home."

"Yes," she said with a oh-so-you-finally-got-it kind of look. "There is no need to go anywhere. We'll go only if it's really important."

If there is nothing important out there why was I wasting my time and energy with unnecessary distractions?

My way of managing my time and energy efficiently is to find pointless distractions, invest in them and deplete my resources, and get badly stuck in the loop. Then, wonder why I have no time or energy left for anything important. Can I train my mind to avoid distracting patterns?

 A Return Gift for You: You achieve more if you stay still and focus on what is important. Conserve your energy for what is important.

63 The Pineapple Juice is Not Good Or Bad

I picked Anjali up after school. She came happily, holding a tetrapack of pineapple juice in her hand. "Today was Brahmani's birthday," she said, "we ate cake, chips and even got this fruit juice."

She sipped from her tetra pack. "This is pineapple," she said.

"Is it nice?" I asked.

"Yes. I like it. But you know we had a big fight today about pineapple juice," she said.

Wow! Why?

"Me and Saketh were standing with our packs when Harish came and told us the pineapple juice is bad. 'How can it be bad?' I asked," said Anjali.

I listened. Where was this leading?

"I told him that he cannot say something like that. How can anything that God gives us be good or bad?" Anjali said.

"Maybe he did not like it," I suggested gently. What's this God business? Was she imposing her views of God on her friends? Was she turning into some kind of religious evangelist?

"If it was bad for him he should say that *he* did not like it. It is *not the pineapple* that is bad. It is he who does not like it. So how can he say it is bad?"

I understood the fine difference in her perception then. There is no good or bad. It is what we make of it. Do not label the object, but instead your reaction to it.

My way of dealing with anything new is to first label it, take a position and defend my position without really knowing what I am defending and why. Then, wonder why life is hard. Can I stop feeling important by passing unnecessary judgements, taking stands I don't need to and imposing my views on others?

A Return Gift for You: You can experience all the shades of life if you do not judge things as good or bad. It's your judgment that makes things good or bad.

64. Computers versus Type Writers

Anjali had never seen a typewriter.

"What are they *Nanna*?" She asked.

I tried to explain. "They are these machines, with keys arranged as in a computer keyboard and rods that connect to the actual letters. We put the paper in, type it out and that is it." She contemplated this.

"You know what that means right?" I asked. "You cannot make a mistake or else you have to type the whole document all over again. Not like a computer on which you can make as many mistakes and then correct them. We had to really *think* before typing. No mistakes."

She thought about what I said for a moment. Then she smiled, terribly pleased with this situation she was in.

"I am so glad we are born now *Nanna*," she said in apparent joy at the conveniences she was enjoying. "I can press delete and undo and write it over again. It's so easy for us."

I was not sure this was where I wanted the conversation to go. But then there was more.

"I wonder what all new things will come when I grow older *Nanna*," she said in genuine wonder and anticipation.

There she stood – looking forward. Flowing. And there I stood – looking back. Stuck.

I can't imagine what will happen to me when the world she is anticipating comes into existence. But with her wonder and joy, I am sure Anjali will have a good time.

My way of choosing between my present and my past is to hold on to and glorify the comforting but dead past, and resist the present, which is alive, here and now. Then, wonder why I have become irrelevant and nothing makes sense to me anymore. Can I be strong enough to let go of the comfortable past and step into the present?

A Return Gift for You: You could look forward and embrace the new as it comes, without being fearful of it. There is no future in being rooted in the past. Life is what's happening now.

65. But You're So Lucky

We were driving to school when I told Anjali I was feeling sleepy.

"Why?" She asked.

"I woke up at three in the morning. Then I worked till 6:30am after which I went for a walk. And now here we are, heading to your school," I said looking for sympathy.

She thought for a while.

"3 o' clock. Wow! You're so lucky *Nanna*. You can do whatever you want, whenever you want."

What?

I hadn't counted myself lucky on that front. Come to think of it, I am fortunate to have so much time at my disposal to use in the manner I want to.

Wonder how many such 'lucky' things I am benefiting from, without my being aware of them?

My way of counting my lucky breaks is to focus exclusively on how unlucky I am and miss all the good luck that I have been privileged to experience all along. Then, wonder when luck will favour me. Can I be aware of my constant good fortune?

A Return Gift for You: You would know how lucky you are if you could see the hidden blessings in every situation, every single time that you feel you are unlucky.

❝❝ Can We Focus on What's Working

Anjali was down with a fever and headache.

"My fever is still there," she said. "But my headache is gone."

"Oh, but why hasn't the fever gone?" I asked. The usual stupid, adult question.

"*Arre* be happy that the headache has gone *na*," she replied in a disappointed tone. "If you keep thinking of why the fever has not gone, even the headache will come back."

It's a universal principle they say. What you focus your attention on, grows. Focus on the good and it becomes better, focus on the bad and it becomes worse.

I spent at least a decade trying to understand this principle. How has she picked it up already?

My way of cheering myself on at work is to worry excessively about what's left to be completed, however little, ignore what has already been achieved, however much, and paint my entire effort as a failure. Then, wonder why I don't achieve as much as I could. Can I stop making life harder for myself?

A Return Gift for You: You can find faster and better results if you train your mind to look at the positives, however miniscule. When you grow those, bit by bit, they will outgrow the negatives. You will find yourself in great space then.

67
Ten Good Things Of The Day

I asked Anjali before she went to sleep if she could recollect ten things that had made her happy during the day. She thought for a moment and started off.

1) I was class monitor (That was fun!)
2) I sat with Brahmani today (That was nice too.)
3) We made a card for Celesta (It was her last day at our school.)
4) Laughed with Mansi (We laughed like crazy!)
5) Played with Shreya (She is fond of Anjali and vice versa.)
6) Helped Akhil write his notes (He speaks awesome English!)
7) Played *kabaddi* (I don't always play but I joined today.)
8) Bought material for making a *rakhi* (Her own initiative.)
9) Made my first *rakhi*.
10) Did 80 laps while skating (She was very proud of the fact.)

"Anything else?" I asked.

Then she said, "Oh, I forgot, I got first prize in the Spelling Bee!"

Of course I already knew about number 11 and was wondering when she would mention it among the good things of her day. But it came almost as an afterthought, perhaps even as a reaction to my 'anything else'. I found it interesting that most things that came to her mind were things that were fun and about her friends. Playing, laughing, helping, making cards, making *rakhis* etc. were happier moments than winning a prize in a competition. Perhaps it would be nice to slide back into life like that where winning competitions takes a back seat to playing with your mates.

My way of identifying the things that make me feel good in my life is to confuse the good with the popular idea of what's good for me, identify with the popular and be unhappy because I am neither happy nor am I popular. Then, wonder why there is no good in my life. Can I choose what's good for me without getting influenced by popular choices?

A Return Gift for You: Your true happiness comes from what really gives you happiness and not from the popular idea of happiness. You choose.

68
Crime and Punishment

Anjali's school starts at 8:30am. But the legion of latecomers who were taking advantage of the student-friendly Daksha School was growing. A circular was issued. Those who come late to school would be sent back. A few days after the circular came into existence, Anjali and I were late by five minutes. I could sense from the deserted road and the officials near the gate that something was not right. I stopped the car.

Anjali was smiling. It was a day before her 'school birthday' and she had many plans with her friends. She was readying herself to step out of the car and into her school's open and welcoming arms. But wait.

I lowered the window to find out. "It's past 8:30," said one of the officials smiling. "We are sending back everyone who is late today."

"So we go back?" I asked to confirm. She smiled and nodded.

Fair enough. Five minutes or one minute, we were late. But the delay was entirely because of me. Anjali was ready well in time. For no fault of hers she had to face the punishment of being sent back. Her teachers are a big deal for her so I wondered how she would react to being sent home by one her favourites.

"Okay, that's a holiday then," I joked as I pulled out. "Let's go home."

But Anjali's face had crumpled. "How can they send me back when I was already in school?" She asked, tears in her eyes. I did not have an answer. She was not at fault. She had gone to school. The same teachers who welcomed her with warm smiles and greetings had sent her away that day. She had every reason to be upset. At the same time, I fully understood the school's desire to enforce discipline.

But I could not help thinking that I was the one who should have been punished because I was the culprit. Anjali is dependent on me after all. How will she understand that the issue is between the school and the parent, and that she got caught in between, and was unfairly punished?

My way of enforcing rules is to interpret rules strictly when I have to apply them to the weakest, and interpret the same rules lightly, when I need to apply them to the strongest, let the culprits go free because they could cause trouble, and punish the

innocents because someone has to be punished for the crime. Then, wonder why there is no justice in the world. Can I find the courage and wisdom to do the right thing and not take the easy way out?

A Return Gift for You: To ensure justice, apply the right principle fairly and consistently without prejudice. Apply the spirit of the law rather than the word. Empathize with the innocent. Put yourself in their shoes. Don't harm the innocent because they have no voice.

69
Spending Time With Myself

"Do you want to go to Mansi's house?" I asked Anjali.

She normally jumps at the idea.

"No," she said.

"Are you sure?" I asked. "I am headed that way. I could drop you."

"I'm sure," she said.

"But what will you do at home? You could play with Mansi," I suggested.

"No," she said. "Today I will spend time with myself. And with Stilton (which was a series of books she was reading those days.)

I had nothing more to say. If I could spend time with myself and be as comfortable, I guess I'd be in pretty good space. It's never too late to change.

My style of treating myself well is to first ensure that I do not listen to myself, do things I don't want to and not do a single thing that I enjoy, for myself. Then, wonder why I am not having a good time. Can I tune in to the soft voice inside me and pay heed to it?

A Return Gift for You: Choose in favour of the soft, intuitive voice inside your head, instead of all the loud voices screaming from the outside. That's your soul calling for your attention. Listen.

70
What Would I Like to Learn

We were driving through Jubilee Hills when we saw a huge hoarding.

'Learn to seize...' screamed an advertisement for a school. It went on about how that educational institution would teach its students how to seize (success perhaps).

Why would an educational institution teach young minds how to seize I wondered. As if we don't have enough seizing and grabbing going on in our world.

"Ha, look at that," said Anjali, quite offended. "Learn to seize?"

I looked at her, wondering what she made of it. 'What would you like to learn?' I asked her.

She thought for a moment,

"I will learn to be kind," she declared.

That's not a bad alternative at all young lady.

If I converted my 'seizing' thoughts into more 'kind' thoughts would I be in a better place? I think I might. So, I vote for kind.

My way of meeting customer needs is to promise what I believe the customer needs, without making any effort to find out what he really needs and blame luck when business goes bad. Then, wonder why the customer is not buying the product I made to meet his need. Can I be true to my customer in a world full of false claims and promises?

A Return Gift for You: You could choose to create the reality you want, the way you want. All else will fall in place when your intent and methods are authentic.

71
Learning to Bicycle

Anjali had her first cycling lesson at a resort that we went to last year. It was a small bike with training wheels. I huffed and puffed alongside, holding her and the bike, as she pedaled away. She liked the experience and we decided to buy her a bicycle so she could learn to ride it.

We bought the bicycle and I promised to teach her to ride it before the summer vacation ended. The first few attempts did not go too well. The training wheels created a problem by coming in the way. The summer vacation ended, I was not happy that I couldn't honour my promise. I extended the deadline by another week. This time I had the training wheels removed, with her consent of course.

I ran beside her manfully as she pedaled away with no sense of balance. The bike veered this way or that and I steadied her and the bicycle with a hand on her shoulder and one on the bike handle. Soon she learned to balance for a few metres on her own. And then some more. Sensing her growing confidence I started to let go bit by bit. "Don't panic," I told her. "Find a way to keep the balance and stay on the bike."

Anjali worked through her fear and finally said, "Give me a start *Nanna* and I will manage this time." She was willing to be on her own, risk a fall and get hurt in the process. Good!

How To Approach Life 179

She appeared confident so I gave her a start and let go. And off she went. I watched her take off, overcoming her panic, finding her freedom as she flew across the road, nay clouds. Just she and her bike. The wings have grown stronger. It was not a bad gift for both of us on Father's Day. A milestone achieved.

My way of attempting to learn new things is to hang on to the comfort of having training wheels, look around for support and give up and fall back on the training wheels when under pressure. Then, wonder why it is difficult to learn even after being so open to learning. Can I risk removing some training wheels in my life too?

A Return Gift for You: To get out of the rut and move ahead faster, check those areas in your life where you still have training wheels on and remove them. Push yourself into the deep end, risk falling and you will learn faster, each time.

72
I Can Learn By Myself – If You Give Me Your Phone

Anjali took a few keyboard lessons from a music teacher – a bike-loving, earring-wearing, real-estate-developing, powder-puffed rebel. But his dominating style of teaching did not appeal to her and she discontinued without making much progress. The keyboard returned to its corner.

On one occasion when we went to pick Anjali from her pal Mansi's house, I requested Mansi's father Ramesh, who plays the keyboard himself, to play his favourite numbers. He played a couple (one from Disco Dancer) and then invited Mansi to play. Mansi played a few themes she had learned with ease. We were effusive in our praise for her performance. Anjali watched quietly.

As soon as we reached home, Anjali asked me for my phone. She removed the covers off the keyboard, Googled 'how to play Tum Hi Ho on keyboard' on YouTube, put the phone in front of her and started playing the keys as instructed. There was not a word about – 'I want a teacher', 'I want to join keyboard classes' nothing. She decided to learn, used the phone to access information and learned how to play the keyboard by herself.

In no time at all, Anjali started playing 'Tum Hi Ho' by herself with no help or encouragement from us. Within the week she was playing tunes like 'Gerua',

'Janam Janam', 'Brown girl in the Ring' and a couple of others. All of them pretty decent to hear. Her guru on YouTube seemed to have done a better job at teaching her than the previous teacher going by the sound of it.

I had heard before how children learn pretty much anything from YouTube these days and become good enough to perform on stage. For instance the performers of 'Rooh' – Shreya, Sruthi, Vivek and Nikhil – the young and energetic band that played at the Vignana Jyothi Institute of Engineering and Technology TEDx event said they learned how to play from YouTube. And they play so well.

With her new found skill, Anjali gave a small performance on the day of her art exhibition.

It's amazing to see how technology has transformed our lives. All limitations of time, money, space, contacts, resources, access have vanished. One phone in hand with access to the Internet and you're in business.

My approach to improve my learning is to want to learn many new things, find limitations everywhere and give up. Then, wonder why technology is so hyped up when I cannot even operate my Smartphone. Can I use technology to change my mindset and my life? Can I be open to the myriad opportunities that technology offers?

A Return Gift for You: You can access anything you want. All limitations are in your mind. There are unlimited opportunities – sitting right there – in your phone. There are no excuses anymore.

Interview With a Six-and-a-Half-Year-Old

We caught up for our half-yearly interview. This time Anjali was not only keen, she was egging me on to do the interview. Her replies were longer and much thought had gone into them to make them more comprehensive for me.

Q. How's life?
A. Good. Interesting. The year is different now. Actually it has been a fun time from January 1st, till today. I hope it stays that way for the rest of the year. I wish that everyone else is happy and they get all things in their life.

Q. What's interesting in life?
A. Most interesting are the new things. Playing badminton.
I actually got the hang of getting up and playing even when I fall or get hurt. Sometimes I get a cut also. It's like I *have* to play. That's all I want to say.

Q. Where did you learn this?
A. You. You only told me when I fell down while playing football.

Q. It's interesting?
A. Because I am learning to do something new.

Q. Why?
A. Because it helps me to continue playing. Or I will stop everything. So the fun stops. The laughing stops and the energy stops. It's just a little pain. Two minutes, and it will go. So I must keep on playing.

Q. What if the pain is too much?
A. If it's bleeding just a dot, then I can play. If the cut is a big one, then I can't play.

Q. What are the fun things?
A. Learning how to skip. So much fun doing that. My birthday last year was great. I don't know why. Chimu Anna was blowing air into balloons and removing it. That was my favourite thing on my birthday.

Q. Any other things?
A. Getting new books. *Mamma* saw something – this book 365 Stories for Boys. Then I found 365 Stories for Girls. Then *Mamma* said she was also looking for the same thing.

Q. What makes you happy?
A. Sitting down in the courtyard. It's airy. Painting – all my memories, my friends and family, having fun with my family and friends. Watching a favourite show or doing something I love to do with them. For example, I love Mythily *attha*. And when I play with her and with my dolls it makes me extra happy.

How To Approach Life 185

Q. What about school?
A. Aerobics first. Sir says I'm not doing well, but I think I am doing it well. Holidays I like. Now when Sankranti holidays come, I will spend the days doing exactly what I like. I got these holidays after thinking so much about them. I like school. I like going. Meeting my friends. Kung fu. I like skating too. kung Fu sir says he will teach me how to break things next year. I don't know how but I like it more each day. On the first day I didn't want kung Fu at all, now I *only* want Kung Fu. I love all my teachers. They teach me so hard. I learn, remember, read it and write it. I have to learn it for my sake. Not for teacher's sake. So it makes me intelligent when I grow up.

Q. What makes you angry?
A. Harsh and Dharini at school. Slight angry. I want to play with Harsh. But Dharini pulls me away from there. Doesn't she understand? I even told *akka* about it. That's one small anger I get. Other thing is when I make small mistakes I don't feel angry. But when *Mamma* shouts at me I get a little angry. But I can't show it. Because then she'll shout even more. So I don't.
I hope *Mamma* is not listening now.

Q. What makes you sad?
A. Most people know I have two friends. Harsh and Mansi. When one of them goes away for two or three days I feel sad. When Chimu Anna goes it's okay. He's busy anyway and I can't force him to stay. But my friends go and I feel bad. I feel bad when I go away

or fall sick. Harsh went away for the whole week and Mansi for one day. So I'm happy she'll be back soon.

Q. What is happiness?
A. What makes us happy. Makes us smile. When we see people or do something with them. Makes us smile. That is happiness. It makes us laugh. So I love happiness. I love laughing.

Q. Why don't you like sadness?
A. It makes me sad. When others come, they also become sad. That's why I don't like it. Even when I am sad. I don't like making others sad. If I could make a list, happiness is first. Sadness is at the end. I don't like sadness.

Q. If God granted you any three things what would you ask for?
A. I'd wish for something that never, never leaves. Something I'll always keep with me. A book. My favourite book. Amar Chitra Katha. Anything that teaches me something. I'd ask for a game maybe. A shop with all the things I like – Tinkle, games that are difficult and make my mind work.

Q. Favourite books?
A. 365 Stories for Girls, BalKand, Mr. Messy Sunnie *mama* bought me big books. I didn't buy them

Q. Who do you like spending time with?
A. Mythily *attha*, Mansi, Harsh, *Mamma*, *Nanna*, Baba, Satish *mama*...

How To Approach Life

Q. What do you think of yourself?
A. I feel I am healthy. In fact I'm an okay type of a girl. A normal girl that lives in the city. I don't know why I get cold and cough. So I think I am doing something wrong. So I am correcting myself to be healthy.

Q. Can I ask you the God question again? If you were to ask God for one thing what would it be?
A. Live a lovely, long life.

Q. What is lovely?
A. Healthy. Long. A joyful life.

Q. What do you think of money?
A. It helps us get our food, be healthy and buy things. We can make it on our own, so we can live a pleasant life. Whenever you have money, collect money. If you don't have a money box put it in any container. So you don't run out of money. That's why I have so many piggy banks.

Q. How can we be happy?
A. Do something you like. Something you love and want to do. Then you'll be happy. Do it with that person you love and trust. Play with them. Help. Or share.

Q. What scares you?
A. Scary jackets.

Q. When did you laugh the most?
A. When you went out, *Mamma* was making funny faces. I laughed the loudest. On January 8th or 9th. It happened twice.

Q. What was the most beautiful thing you saw?
A. Tree. Blooming with purple. I didn't even know that there were purple trees (trees with purple flowers). Somewhere in the colony.

Q. Anything else you want to add?
A. No

Q. What are your Sankranti vacation plans?
A. Spend time with friends. Go out with my friends. Out of this city – slightly (obviously not with friends but with family hopefully). Some nearby place like a beach.

Me: Thank you Anjali for the interview.

Anjali: Can I say something? Interview is the thing I wanted to do. I like answering questions. I like to do it with my Dad.

Q. Why?
A. Because he is good on the computer. And funny.

So ended my interview with Anjali. I loved her advice on saving money. I think I'll follow that. Also on being happy – do what you love. With people you love and trust.

She was keen to go on but I could not think of too many questions to ask. Also, my hand was aching from too much writing.

PART 5

HOW TO GET THINGS DONE

73
How To Play a Game Right

Anjali invited me to play a board game. We had to pick letters and numbers from a box, match them with those on the board. Whoever finishes first wins the game. Aha. A game! Competition!

I played in deadly earnest. I seized all the letters of the alphabet that came my way. I kept a wary eye on Anjali's progress.

Anjali's approach was different though. She did not wait for her turn. Instead, she flipped the cards to look for what she needed. "I need a *Nanna*!" She announced and started searching for it. She found that I had an unused A. "*Nanna*, I need that A!" she exclaimed as if I was illegally hoarding all the As in the world. I let her have it.

Then she noticed that she had something that I needed. She passed it on to me, her opponent. "*Nanna*, here is a P," and so on. The game progressed rapidly under these new cooperative rules. From the corner of my eye I noticed (unhappily) that she was almost done. I searched desperately for pieces to finish my game. Anjali sensed my desperation and postponed her victory to help me out. "Here is an A, a U… hey even I need a U…" and so on. And even as she helped me first, she managed to finish her game. It was time for high-fives!

I could not help noticing how focused I had been on finishing my game, to the extent of ignoring her. But she was open to doing her thing, and also seeing that her *Nanna* needed help. When I had something she needed, it was only by the third game that I gave it to her first; something she had been happily doing all along. If she needed a letter, and I needed it as well, she would give it to me first. She gave, again and again, until I got over my fear of losing, my lack of trust in the process, and started reciprocating. And she was as happy at my finishing the game as she was with hers.

It looks like we can all win. Not necessarily only one of us. And I also realized one more thing. When I consciously helped her find the N that she so badly needed, I found an N that I needed too.

Competing is one thing but winning by pulling the other down is another. Compete hard, but be open to help. The journey gets better. You get richer.

My style of competing is to win at all costs and in the process throw all principles of honesty, fairness and justice out of the window. Then, wonder why I don't like it when my

opponents win by using the same tactics against me. Can I be aware of my fears and insecurities about winning and losing?

 A Return Gift for You: If you want to win, compete without the fear of losing. Then you will understand how to play to win.

74
The Power of Three Boons

Anjali revealed this secret to me. "I realized we get three boons each day," she whispered to me just before she went to sleep. "So now I ask for three boons everyday. It could be going to the sand pit at school or anything simple like that."

"Oh," I said. That simple huh? Ask for three boons everyday?

"Then, after the three boons are over, I ask the opposite machine (some imaginary machine it looks like, that gives you the opposite of what you want)," she said. "That's because after the three boons are given, we start getting the opposite of what we ask. So I ask for the opposite of what I want. I realized that after the first few times."

I don't know how to deal with the opposite machine (which seems to be working overtime in my case), but the three boons a day technique seems like a powerful tool. Imagine having three simple boons to ask for everyday. It would help me think more creatively and think of better outcomes. I scare myself to death with negative thoughts anyway.

I used the three-boon-technique the next day. I ended up asking for one boon, which indicates how reluctant I am to create what I want in my life. (I'd rather be handed stuff I don't want and complain about it than make an effort to ask for it.) My one boon was granted too!

I asked Anjali if I could share this information with others so they could ask for three boons too. She agreed. So we can all go ahead.

My way of asking life for what I want from it is to present a list of scary scenarios I think up every morning, get scared with my own creations, then get stressed when told that I could have asked for good outcomes instead. Then, wonder why I can't seem to think of any good outcomes. Can I train my mind to ask for my good?

A Return Gift for You: You could ask for three things everyday. All you have to do is ask. You could train your mind to visualize and imagine the best possible outcomes. What you can see in your mind is what can get.

75
The Secret Formula for Success

I was running races with Anjali and as usual, lost them all. She turned to me and said, "It's okay *Nanna*, just keep practicing. You will win sometime."

I nodded. We raced again.

After a couple of races, I caught up with her. She gave me a wry, knowing smile. "See? Practice." I don't get to win either way!

We sat down after a while, tired. I asked her how she figured out how to win.

"I know how to win *Nanna*!" She declared confidently.

"How?" I asked eagerly.

"Keep trying *Nanna*," she said simply.

Thanks Coach. I will.

My way of wanting success is to put in minimal effort, fail, give up and find something else quickly because if I try for longer and fail, it will be admitting failure. Then, wonder why I am not successful at anything. Can I get past my comfortable relationship with failure? And my fear of success?

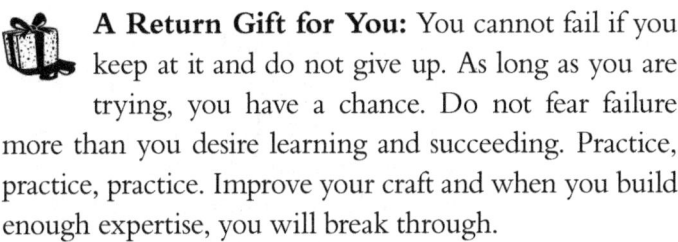 **A Return Gift for You:** You cannot fail if you keep at it and do not give up. As long as you are trying, you have a chance. Do not fear failure more than you desire learning and succeeding. Practice, practice, practice. Improve your craft and when you build enough expertise, you will break through.

76
Are Snakes Ladders Too

Anjali and I were playing Snakes and Ladders. She was in no hurry. She plodded along and counted out the number of moves on her fingers. I was getting worked up on the other side of the board. For me, the snakes were my enemies and the ladders, my greatest pals. (And, my happy-go-lucky opponent, my foe.)

We were even initially. Then I surged ahead thanks to my good friends, the ladders. In fact, I was just one move away from finishing the game in style. Victory was in sight!

The last time we had played, months ago, Anjali had beaten me soundly. Looks like things have changed now. But wait a minute. Why was she enjoying herself more?

While I was riding on my ladders and going upwards, Anjali encountered a series of large snakes that set her back considerably. "Wheee" she shouted happily. "I am going down," as if they were gigantic slides. One time she slipped from 90 to 3 and she seemed elated to get a double ride down on two long snakes! I could not understand that because every time a snake caught me, I felt victimized. I was like "why me?" But for her, snakes and ladders were the same thing – great fun to climb up or slide down.

As luck would have it, a vile, cunning snake, gobbled me up when I was on 98, two points away from a famous win. I slid right down to the bottom. Anjali meanwhile slipped and slid so many times that I thought she would never ever get back into the game.

But she was not bothered. She actually found time to encourage me enthusiastically. Some 'whees' and 'wows' livened up her side of the board and I noticed that she had progressed a bit. Some tragic turns of fate at my end and I slid further down. "I need a three," she announced suddenly, threw the dice, got a three, finished the game and smiled. "It's okay *Nanna*," she said with her now customary advice to me. "Keep on trying." It seemed like a 'Keep on crying' moment for me though.

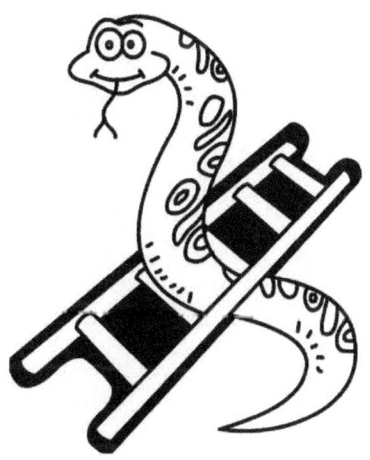

I'd do anything for an attitude like that – to be able to look at a game as a game and enjoy it, to see both snakes and ladders as my friends, to enjoy the downs as 'whee' moments. When I am happy, I court luck.

I remember playing a game called 'Satori' in a workshop. The game reflects our consciousness uncannily. Just as life does. It taught me that to improve my consciousness, I could get out of the way, trust the process, do things I am expected to do and mostly surrender.

My way of dealing with the 'good' and 'bad' is to first label things using my fine discretion, then avoid the 'bad', court only the 'good' and thereby, miss a lot of 'good' in the 'bad'. Then wonder why life's not giving me enough good opportunities. Can I treat ups and downs equally?

A Return Gift for You: You could enjoy life so much more if you could 'Whee' on every down that you encounter and encourage others while you are on your way up. It's a game you can never lose. Wheeeee!

77. Lessons from a Soccer Game

It's soccer time. Anjali and I were kicking a plastic Mickey Mouse ball. She was fully involved in the game – making and changing rules, improvising techniques and most importantly, giving me her *gyan*.

I was forewarned by her that she was to win, so I made sure I stuck to her rules. Noticing that she had kicked in more goals than me and observing my wayward kicks, the four-year-old stopped the game and told me the first rule. "*Nanna*, you should aim and kick. Otherwise it will go here and there. Aim at the goal and then it will go there." So true. (Most times I don't even know what my goal is.)

We continued playing. Anjali was scrapping hard for the ball and kicking it with lots of gusto. She took a breather to tell me what she was doing right (obviously her tally of goals was even higher now). "*Nanna*, see why I am getting more points. I am kicking and kicking and kicking and kicking. You should also keep kicking." Okay Coach, never stop the action and keep at it.

She heard me appreciating a strong kick she had executed. "Stop cheering me *Nanna*," she admonished me, "cheer yourself. Otherwise you will never win." Oops. Keep the focus on yourself and keep motivating yourself instead of getting distracted.

But I could not resist telling her that she really was putting a lot of effort into her kick and that was why I appreciated it. She nodded, thinking that perhaps I was now ready to imbibe the secret behind kicking the ball well. "Just keep looking at the ball and kick at it. Look closely at the ball. Don't look here and there." There was a bit of technical insight too on how I should take a small run up and kick the ball hard.

I was standing near my goal waiting for the ball to come my way. "Don't simply stand there," she said. "Keep moving."

And the last of my coach's words of wisdom from the football game. "And think, *Nanna*. It is a thinking game."

She gave me credit for the last one, "you told me remember, when I was crying after I lost in chess, that it is a thinking game! I am just telling you what you told me."

How To Get Things Done

I smiled at my young teacher, happy that she gave me credit where due. And with that, we wound up a long and hard game of football. I, as usual, ended up losing the game, but gained a lot of wisdom from a willing, caring and spontaneous teacher – aim at the goal, keep scrapping, don't 'just stand there', cheer yourself, look closely at the ball, keep moving and keep thinking.

Thanks Coach.

Can I take the same attitude to life that I use in a game?

A Return Gift for You: You could find goal clarity, aim at the goal, keep moving, cheer yourself, keep focus on what you are doing and keep thinking all the time. Missed any?

78 We Play Fully When We Play a Match

It was shuttle-badminton time. Anjali had improved quite a bit and was playing increasingly longer rallies with me so I suggested we play a game.

"A game?" She asked, surprised that she had graduated to playing a game with me already.

I shrugged.

"Let's play," I said. "What's the big deal?"

After a few points, the competitive spirit kicked in and Anjali was fighting hard to win points.

She realized it too.

"When we play a match we play more fully no *Nanna*," she observed after a hard rally.

Yes Anjali. It's the oldest way to get people involved. Throw them a challenge. Make them compete against time and against others. Then we play 'fully'. (It also indicates that at other times, we do not play 'fully'.)

Challenge and interest go together. When team members are not 'fully' interested, it's the mentor's, coach's job to create an interesting challenge. If there's no one to challenge us, it's in our own interest to challenge ourselves and engage more 'fully'.

My way of challenging myself is to put in effort that's way below my best because it's cool to do it without much effort, be

surprised that I failed to achieve what I wanted, refuse to put in more effort, find work boring because I am failing and stop challenging myself further. Then, wonder why my job is boring. Can I understand that life is most interesting when I do my best?

A Return Gift for You: To achieve your potential, look to challenge yourself everyday, every hour. You could perk your life up with small wins, small victories and make your work and life that much more rewarding.

79
Do Things You Don't Like First

Anjali came home from school. After the usual chat about her friends and what they did at school, she turned her attention to the 'lots of homework' she had to do. The mood turned despondent, but she strode purposefully into her room to get her school bag.

She returned and announced loudly, "I don't like Math."

"There's too much work in Math – I have to write 81, 82, 83, 84 and 85 three times each," she explained. I wondered what I ought to do to revive her interest in Math. This wouldn't do.

Before I could say anything and spoil it all she sat with her Math book writing her 81s, 82s and 83s. I remained silent. What now?

After the work was done to satisfaction, she looked at me and said *"Nanna,* what I don't like, I finish first. That way it won't be there later."

I wish I'd known that earlier. I would have got rid of much stuff that I don't like by now. Instead it's still there with me, waiting to be addressed. A lot of baggage.

My way of doing things efficiently is to put off the important and difficult things for later, do the unimportant jobs first, tire myself out after engaging in useless activities and postpone

what's important. Then, wonder why there is so much left to be done and why life feels heavy. Can I stop postponing my good?

A Return Gift for You: You could make serious progress if you address the difficult and important jobs first. The phone call. The email. The query letter. Get it done with. Now.

80 Taking the High Performance Route at Golconda

We were at Golconda fort on a hot, summer morning. We chose a route with steep granite steps that lead straight to the top. It was a 25–minute climb at least. I mentally prepared myself to carry Anjali – there was no way she would go up the steep climb in the heat.

After a few steps I paused and waited for her to ask to be carried. She did not. Instead, she walked halfway up the hill on her own. At the next break, some warrior spirit awakened within her and she said to me, her face resolute – "I will not give up. I will climb all the way to the top."

One look at her face and I knew that she would do it, that's how determined she was. And climb she did, and in good humour, cracking a few jokes here and there. There was a moment of weakness when she was about to complain. But she caught herself, reminded herself and me – "I will not give up". She climbed the entire distance on her own.

On the way down she complained a bit but then decided she would climb down on her own too. I must however carry her when we get to the flat area. I agreed.

It's that decision, that 'click' in our mind that sparks the critical, creative part of our lives. All champions talk of that moment when they 'decided' that they would rather die than give up. Only after that decision was made did they focus entirely on the process, eliminate all distracting thoughts, and achieve the goals they set for themselves. This interests me no end because all of us have the capability to decide, commit and execute those big performances as often as we can, in things that matter most to us.

My way of handling a really tough challenge is to start with weak and tentative desire, weaken it further with constant doubt, imagine ways that I could fail, scare myself further and give up on the challenge bit by bit. Then, wonder what else I should have done to achieve my big goals. Can I take up bigger challenges more often for my own growth?

A Return Gift for You: You could achieve performances that are ten times your average performance if you decide and commit to it. Whenever your mind tells you to stop, don't. Keep going. After each goal is achieved, embark on something bigger. Slow down, but don't stop.

81 A New Definition of a Loser

After inventing a few new words like 'highover' (flyover) and some others that I cannot remember right now, Anjali came up with a new way to look at the word 'loser'.

"I am not a loser," she said yesterday after losing a badminton game, "I am a finder."

Someone who loses need not be a loser. Instead, she could be a finder. One who is finding ways to improve oneself even in failure. It fits in with the growth mindset.

I love this new perspective.

Fellow losers of the world – hear it now! You are all finders. As long as you remain finders, you will hit the high road. It's just a matter of perspective.

My way of dealing with failure is to throw everything away after losing, including the valuable lesson it came wrapped in and repeat the same mistake again and again. Then, wonder why I keep failing. Can I take home something – a lesson, if not the trophy?

A Return Gift for You: When you nurture the learning mindset you will always be a winner.

When all seems lost don't give up – look for the valuable lesson. Every loss is a temporary setback if you learn the lesson.

82. Add Challenge to Boring Jobs

We were playing cricket. Anjali was batting. She got bored after a while.

"I like to hit the ball hard," she said, "so I will hit the ball even if I get out. Okay?"

All focus shifted to hitting the ball. After a few robust hits, she stopped. I could see she was bored with her hitting the ball routine.

"I like to run. Can I run?" She asked adding yet another challenge.

"Of course," I said, "every time you hit the ball, you can run. Don't get run out though."

She liked my challenge.

Now all focus was on scoring runs. She changed her batting style a bit. She focused on getting bat to ball and ran a single or a double on every ball. The energy in the arena increased with these constant changes and challenges. We ran around much more, shouting, yelling and laughing, which wouldn't have been, if she had not added challenge to the game. A good lesson in how to make boring jobs interesting.

Another time, Anjali was doing her homework – boring work! She asked me for my phone.

"In how many minutes should I complete this problem?"

"Five minutes," I replied.

"Okay," she said.

She started the timer, gave me the phone and went on doing her homework. I looked at the timer as it headed towards zero, the seconds ticking away rapidly. I found myself getting tense and excited as the seconds went by. I counted down the minutes for her. It was like watching a close game of cricket.

The moment any activity falls into a routine we could add challenge and do things differently. It's a simple way to make life more fun and exciting.

My way of making work interesting is to wait for it to become exciting on its own, get bored when it does not, stop activity, look for someone to liven work up for me, get bored again, give up, and fare badly as a result of all the bored work. Then, wonder why work is so boring. Can I understand that it's not the work that's boring, but my attitude to it?

 A Return Gift for You: To make life (and work) interesting, do things differently, innovate and challenge yourself every moment.

83
The Happy Rakhi Day Startup

Anjali participated in her annual *rakhi*-making competition at school a couple of days before the actual day. She told me that she had never won any a prize for this particular craft in all these years. "But this year I will win," she said with a determined look. With a little preparation and a simple idea she managed a third prize. This was a big deal and she was happy with the result. (She was also happy that her *akka* had told her before the prizes were announced that she suspected Anjali might win the first prize – for her, which was as good as winning the first prize.)

Back at home, she showed me her creation and told me how simple her idea was and how detailed and complex the other *rakhis* were. She was all praise for the winner who had crafted an elaborate *rakhi* by sticking grains and things like that. "Aunty said that she was giving marks mainly for the effort that went into making the *rakhi*," she said happily.

Sometime soon her business idea developed.

"*Nanna*, why don't I make *rakhis* for all the *atthas* (her aunts)?" She asked. "They have to buy *rakhis* for you and *Pappa* anyway." Off we went to the bookshop where she meticulously chose the kind of paper she wanted – ribbons, Fevicol and other such materials. Suitably armed with the raw material, we then headed off to her favourite *aunt*, Mythily *attha's* house where the *rakhi* manufacturing process began in right earnest.

Anjali needed to get four *rakhis* for her cousins plus eight for her aunts. Twelve *rakhis* in all. She recruited technical expertise from two of her *atthas* and got eight *rakhis* done on Day One. The remaining four were completed the next day. The prices were fixed – the complex *rakhis* at Rs. 50 and the simple ones at Rs. 10. All aunts were informed that no outside *rakhis* need be bought since they had already been made. Sealed in a box like the Finance Minister's budget, the *rakhis* made their way home amidst tight security that night.

The *rakhis* were put on display on D day. Money changed hands briskly as Anjali went about comfortably selling them at a 100 bucks a pair. By the end of the day the enterprising little miss grossed well over 2,500 (most were bought at a premium) which went straight into her notes bank.

To her credit, the *rakhis* did look different and colourful and I enjoyed wearing them all day. Her *atthas* were thrilled to be a part of the project and planned bigger events in the future. They were more than happy with the *rakhis* and the event and showed their happiness by paying her large premiums.

Looking back, her successful venture had many principles of business management working for it. The idea of making *rakhis* to meet a clear gap in the market was conceived well in advance. To deal with the increased scale of operations she recruited help – me to buy the material and her *atthas* to manufacture the *rakhis* – and kept us interested and motivated by promising us Rs. 5 each. She offered two variants, positioned and priced them separately. She advertised the product to all her possible customers by calling each one of them. When they arrived, she was ready with a nice display on a big table, and completed the business end of the venture.

My way of managing a business is to identify a market need, mull over it, talk about the opportunity with others, do nothing about it and watch someone else step in and make a killing. Then, wonder why I am not getting lucky breaks while all others are. Can I act decisively and instantly when I am seized by an idea and seek help when I need it to implement it well?

A Return Gift for You: You could run a profitable venture if you applied the principles of common sense to your work. You could get the job done to satisfaction if you lead the effort and manage your team well. But there's no escaping the responsibility – it's your baby.

84
I'll Beat Yasvantt Someday

Every Saturday Anjali goes to a skating class. Her friend Yasvantt also comes to the same skating class which motivates her I guess. She tries hard to compete with a group of boys in the class, some of them who are really good. Yasvantt is one of the stronger skaters in the group so he leaves her far behind and overtakes her in the succeeding laps too.

I wondered how she would handle this. Not being as good as the others in the group can be demotivating. Though she is the only girl in the group, she does not take too kindly to losing.

But week after week she prods me to take her to the skating sessions. It's the same routine each time. We go to class. She goes to the coach, wishes him, gets ready and asks Yasvantt to race her in a warm-up run. Yaswantt beats her easily. But she puts in all her effort.

Then comes the skating. Same story. She is somewhere at the end of the line. But she comes away happy, and always with good news – I beat that new girl, or I came second today in that lap. The look on her face is one of intense concentration as she completes her laps. Sometimes the effort is worth it, other times it's not. But she bears it and most times focuses on her small improvements or on something that happened to laugh at.

After one such session, she challenged Yasvantt again. "Race?" she asked. "Yes," he said. Off they went, the two of them and another boy. The boys took off like hares with Anjali in hot pursuit. And then, disaster. Her shoe came off midway.

For a while, she tried to run with one shoe and then realised it wasn't working. Then she tried to quickly put on her shoe in an attempt to catch up with them. But by then, they were back.

I wondered how she'd react to this twist of fate. It looked tragic, she standing there with the shoe in hand as the boys walked back. But she shrugged it off and told the other two that it had come off. Then she came to me and I tied her laces again. She returned to the fray.

"Race?" She asked.

Yasvantt was game again. The young boy shot off, striding powerfully ahead. Anjali followed all intent and effort as she tried to catch up but ended a distant second.

"Someday," she said in the car, her face resolute, "I will beat him." I nodded.

My approach to competing with the best in my class is to avoid them because they make me look bad in comparison, refuse to compete with them because I don't want to lose, drop off and join a class with a lower standard where I become the best so I can feel better. Then, wonder why I am not improving. Can I keep going at it, loss after loss after loss, until I win?

A Return Gift for You: You could deal with tough competition by using it as an opportunity to grow. Better competition sets the bar high and gives you an opportunity to compete against better players. When you hang in there through the discomfort, you will learn the right things much faster.

85
Organizing My Birthday Party

Anjali's birthday was approaching fast and there was the familiar excitement in the air. Who to invite, what to eat, gifts and all the rest. It's usually a pretty large affair so planning starts a week in advance. However gifts for her must not be mentioned – 'I want a surprise.'

I did not realize how serious Anjali was about her birthday party until I saw three printed sheets pinned to my board. The first sheet was a list of all her guests which included her entire class, all 17 of them. The second sheet had a list of games to be played on the day. The third was a list of articles that needed to be bought – snacks, cake, return gifts etc. On the list of friends, Mansi had already been assigned some responsibility.

Considering the detail with which she is planning for her birthday party, I will not be surprised if she comes up with a comprehensive how-to-organize-my-birthday-party manual complete with roles, responsibilities, schedules and backup plans by next year.

For me, birthdays are days that happen, like life, and you handle them the best you can as they come. Makes me wonder, if I had been half this prepared and organized, I probably would have done something with myself. But good for you Anjali; this is certainly a lesson

I will take seriously from now onward. Like someone said, you must work to ensure your happiness.

My way of preparing for a happy event is to desire the best experience, do nothing about it, but hope someone else does it and then blame everyone when nothing happens. Then I wonder why my happy events end up unhappily. Can I ensure happiness for myself simply because I love myself and deserve it?

A Return Gift for You: If you want a happy time in your life, plan and organize for your happiness just as you plan and organize for the other areas of your life. Don't take chances with your happiness and expect it to happen on its own.

86

Performing Without Pressure

We were playing badminton. Anjali said "Let's play longer rallies *Nanna*." I agreed.

We focused on playing longer rallies and congratulated one another whenever a long rally was achieved. After a few such long rallies, she stopped and made an observation.

"When we think we should play long rallies, we are not able to do them. But when we play freely we get longer rallies," she said.

I nodded.

When I attach myself to the outcome, I take my focus off the process and cannot perform at my best. I am better off putting all my focus into hitting the shuttle. When I am fully involved in the process, I perform better and am bound to have longer rallies anyway.

Of course playing freely does not mean being casual. It is about focusing on what I can control, and minimizing unnecessary burdens like worrying about outcomes which are not in my control. Achieving the outcome happens to be a by-product.

My way of achieving my goal is to want the result badly, ignore the process, perform poorly, stress myself about not achieving the goal and fail. Then, wonder what went wrong

because I did everything right. Can I keep my focus on the process to the extent that I forget the outcome?

A Return Gift for You: You could handle pressure by staying in the present, and focusing on the process. Focusing on the outcome adds unwanted pressure on you because you cannot control it. Focus on what you can control and you will feel no pressure.

87 I'll Learn From My Mistakes the Hard Way

We were playing chess. Anjali made a mistake and lost her queen. It was an important stage in the game so I asked her if she wanted to replay it.

"No, I want to play like a real game," she said emphatically, despite her disappointment.

I insisted, saying "It's okay. You are learning anyway. Replay it and see if you can play it differently this time."

But she was adamant.

"No. I will learn from my mistakes."

Okay. It's the most effective way to learn I guess. Set the bar high. Don't take easy exit routes. Look your mistakes in the eye. Correct the process. It is the way to learn faster.

My way of improving my skill is to avoid tough challenges, ponder over how things can be done in a 'smart' way by putting less effort and lower my standards subsequently. Then, wonder why I am not making it to the top bracket. Can I train myself to take the toughest way to learn?

A Return Gift for You: You could hasten your learning process many times over by taking setbacks head on and figuring out how to get past them. It's painful but effective.

88 The 'Lucky Lemons' Lemonade Stall

"I will set up a lemonade stall," Anjali declared, "I will sell lemonade."

Visions of Dennis the Menace and Joey, and their lemonade stalls flashed through my head. I looked on silently – any comment here could create problems for me.

"I will call Mansi and we will make lemonade and sell it outside and make money," Anjali said. She seemed convinced that she has to fend for herself and that she might have to do a better job of it than relying on us for money.

"Okay," I said. Let me say yes for a change.

"Yay," she yelled excitedly and disappeared.

I left her to ponder over the idea. Obviously she would need help at some stage. I wanted to see at what stage she would involve me.

Anjali's business venture was launched that same afternoon by unveiling her brand 'Lucky Lemons' through a poster. She conceptualized it, wrote the copy and designed it. 'Lucky Lemons' had a visual of a smiling lemon sipping lemonade stylishly with a straw. The rest of the poster advertised a Buy-Two-Get-One offer, two variants of lemonade with or without ice, and their prices. An invitation to 'Come In' rounded off the thoughtful advertisement. Very cool indeed.

"Will you help me put up the table and chair at 4 'o clock?" She asked.

"Yes," I said. She obviously knew who was fit for what job. Only the physical and menial jobs for me.

Meanwhile Anjali got busy with Shobha to make the lemonade. She got ice cubes, two separate jugs for iced lemonade and normal lemonade, some cookies and was all set.

It was time for the table and chair. "Do you want it outside the gate?" I asked. Since her friend Mansi was not coming, Anjali would have to manage her stall alone.

"What about dogs?" She worried. These days there are many strays that go around in packs in the colony and she was aware of that. I suggested that she could set up the stall inside the gate and leave the gate open.

She promptly stuck the poster on the gate. There was lemonade and cookies on sale. The stall was open.

I like lemonade. More so when Anjali is selling it. So I drank up a few glasses and ate some cookies. Her *Ajji* visited the Lucky Lemons stall and so did her cousin Chimu. After Anjali pocketed some Rs. 130, she closed shop for the day.

In case some customers dropped in after hours and got disappointed, she wrote with a chalk on the gate. "Closed. Come again next Saturday." On the floor nearby, the logo was drawn – lemonade with a cocky mug and a rakishly angled straw. The loop was closed.

The idea of an unmet demand in the market, then the right product to satisfy the need – lemonade in two variants, with and without ice started it off. Then came the pricing at Rs. 10 (without ice), Rs. 15 (with ice) and cookies at Rs. 15. The brand name of 'Lucky Lemons' was peppy, fun and easy to remember. The logo of a lucky lemon drinking lemonade from a mug was as good as they come. An attractive deal of getting one free if you bought two, to entice more business. The mantra of advertising – repetition of the message was diligently followed – on the poster, the floor, the wall. I know I compromised her on the place (the stall on the pavement outside would have doubled her sales). I guess it rounds off all the Ps of marketing – Product, Price, Promotion and Place – and more.

She already has some new ideas, "I will sell to those uncles who play badminton everyday," she told me. I think I should make her my agent. Problem is – I don't think she will accept me as her client. She has pretty clear ideas on that.

My approach to marketing and branding my business activity is to think of an idea, dream about it, close the idea and move on to the next idea. Then, wonder why my business ideas are not taking off. Can I risk putting my ideas out there more honestly to give them a chance?

A Return Gift for You: You could get most things right in your business if you are fully focused on satisfying the customer. All other things will fall in place if you keep your customer in sight. Be close to your customer.

Imagine There is Nothing to Do, Then Pick One

"I have so many things to do Anjali," I complained, "what do I do?"

We were walking in the supermarket. There were several things pending on my desk, all seemingly important and urgent.

"Stop worrying about all those things," she said, "imagine you have nothing to do."

I made a face.

"Then how will I get any work done?" I asked.

"Pick one job. Think that it is the only one you have and complete it. And after that pick the next one. That way you have only one job at a time and you will not worry about having too many."

This made immense sense. I asked suspiciously. "Who told you that?"

"No one," she laughed and went back to her normal mischievous self. "Okay, now you can stop imagining."

In a situation that overwhelms, pick the most important job and do it. Nothing else. Hmm.

It is popular legend how Andrew Carnegie of US Steels told a management consultant Frederick Taylor that he would pay $10,000 (in 1890) if Taylor could give him management advice worth listening to. Taylor replied that Carnegie should make a list of ten most important things he had to do and start doing number one. Carnegie paid him $10,000. So the story goes.

My way of dealing with pending jobs is to pile them up, fret a lot, distract myself with unimportant jobs, feel pressured, fret some more and then give up. Then, wonder why nothing gets done and why the pending jobs are still pending. Can I focus on one job at a time and do it as if it's the only job I have?

A Return Gift for You: You could bring great efficiencies to your job if you take up one important task at a time, and complete it well, instead of doing many minor tasks. Focus your mind, don't distract it.

90
Finish the Job First, Smile Later

We were playing badminton again. After a long rally Anjali mishit a shot and stopped to analyze why she did that.

"When I smile in the middle of the rally, my concentration goes," she observed.

Aha!

Does that mean that a distracting thought entered her head making her lose focus and thereby mishit the shuttlecock? Many times I have observed that I tend to distract myself from the process by congratulating myself too early, or admonishing myself for a small error, and lose my rhythm. This, I do, even before the rally has ended. Consequently I lose the point.

Okay next time, no distracting thoughts. Just focus on work.

My way of closing out any job well is to sniff the advantage, congratulate myself before the job is fully done, celebrate the win in my head, lose focus, give up my advantage and lose the game. Then, wonder why I am unlucky. Can I hold my complete concentration until the job is fully done?

A Return Gift for You: To end on a winning note, focus on the process until the job is done and delivered. Any distraction, internal or external, can change the result in a matter of moments, and all your hard work goes waste.

91
Using Feedback to Learn Faster

Anjali told me there was a marked improvement in the English speaking ability of her class.

"Earlier some of us would say 'buyed' for 'bought' or 'back of you' for 'behind you'. But now they are all speaking good English. Lot of improvement," she said happily.

"How come?" I asked her curious to know.

"Chandana aunty told us to correct one another," she said. "When someone makes a mistake anyone of us can correct them immediately. That's why we are not making the same mistakes again."

Wow! It's such an elegant way to share knowledge and apply corrections instantly. It involves everyone at all times, not just the teacher during the class time and hastens the learning process. It's such a creative thought. Just look at the results!

Adults rarely call out one another's mistakes for fear of upsetting the other. If we called out when someone was making an error or even when they are doing things right, the team builds a wonderful culture and it becomes a powerful self-correcting mechanism.

Good for you Chandana aunty for enabling the instant feedback mechanism and making learning such a fun experience.

My method of enabling faster learning in the team is to retain all power with myself, restrict information sharing and prevent team members from correcting one another because I don't trust their ability to do so. Then, wonder why the class is not progressing fast enough. Can I drop my 'I know everything' attitude and be open for correction? And to correct others?

A Return Gift for You: You could enable faster and more effective learning among your team members by utilizing every resource available. All you have to do is empower each resource you have and they become little extensions of you.

92
Let's Go Jogging

I told Anjali I was going to the park for my run. After many years I had gradually increased my 100-metre run and had now progressed to one kilometre.

Anjali wanted to come with me and appeared in her sports shoes. I was surprised. I thought she would sit around in the lawns and watch the birds and flowers.

"I want to run with you *Nanna*," she said.

I told her to run as much as she could and break off whenever she wanted to. I would run the great distance of 1 km at my own pace.

"Okay," she said and ran alongside me.

She ran faster than I did, came running back, caught up with me again, and chatted me up.

"I won't be able to talk much," I huffed and puffed. "I need to save my breath."

"Oh," she said and ran off. She came back again.

"You're not lifting your knees high enough," she told me. "Take bigger strides."

I grimaced. If I could raise those knees higher, I would have.

"Look at me," she said, showing how easily she was doing it. I grimaced again.

After a while I told her. "Okay, if you're tired, stop."

"No, I will run," she said even though she had tired a bit. She walked alongside me, fell back a bit, ran and caught up with me, fell back and kept coming.

After some more time I told her to take it easy. This time she was not happy.

"*Arre*, I am running no. Let me run. Why do you want to stop me?"

I suddenly realized what I was doing. I was giving her the easy way out. I assumed that she could not handle it. But not only did she finish the entire distance ahead of me – run and walk – she also had some tips and insights for me.

"Run slowly on the down slopes *Nanna*," she said. "They take more energy."

Later, we sat on the steps.

"I am sweating like a pig," she said smiling. We both enjoyed the exhilaration one gets after a good run. It's a lovely feeling of satisfaction, contentment and achievement when sweat pours down. And she almost did not experience it, thanks to me. How many times do I take that pleasure away from her I wonder?

I was surprised at her stubborn attitude to finishing the distance, despite her tired and stumbling manner in the end. There's so much children bring to the table and we block them again and again. Learn to back off!

My way of dealing with tough challenges is to mentally compromise at the first opportunity, buy into distracting feedback and quit before I give it my best shot. Then, wonder why I didn't make it with my talent. Can I be genuinely supportive of others growth? Can I stop hindering their growth with my fears and my ego?

A Return Gift for You: You grow others by helping them to go past their limits; not by limiting them with your fears – disguised as love. Step back and allow them space to grow if you really love them.

Interview with a Seven-Year-Old

I had been putting this interview off for a while but the other evening Anjali barged into my room and said. 'Interview.'

I said "two minutes." But no, it had to be right now. And so it started.

Q. Now you're seven. How do you feel?
A. Haaappyyy!

Q. So what have you done in your seven years?
A. Gone to Goa, and I am not scared of getting into the water now at the beach. Also for the first time I called more than two friends for my birthday.

Q. What do you like the most?
A. Tinkle Digest. *Nanna and Amma*.

Q. What's the happiest thing that happened last year?
A. Diwali *mela* at school. It was so much fun for me. There was a haunted house, so much food, and *diyas* and masks.

Q. What's your favourite food?
A. (After a lot of thought.) Maybe ice cream.

Q. What do you like to read?

A. Suppandi, Shikari Shambhu, Eena Meena Myna Moh, I have a dream, Ramu and Shamu and other funny tales. Princess Adventure books. All adventure stories.
Q. You like adventure?
A. Yeah. It is all about bravery. And my favorite tale in that was Runaway Rajah.

Q. What does bravery mean to you?
A. Being bold. Not being scared. You can face anything. Lizards also.

Q. Do you think you are brave?
A. Maybe not. Sometimes I think I am. Sometimes I am not. When I see lizards, I get all freaked out.

Q. When do you feel you are brave?
A. Once *na*, I made a ugly lizard with clay. Amma and all were scared. I was just saying what is so scary about it.

Q. Is it okey to be scared?
A. Yup. There's nothing that says you cannot be scared.

Q. What makes you happy?
A. Being at school with all my friends. Going to birthday parties because you get so much cake to eat. I asked for two pieces of cake at Harsh's birthday party.

Q. What makes you sad?
A. (Makes a sad face.) Mostly nothing except if someone shouts at me. Or like on my birthday Shiny broke my crayons. Or when my friends go out of town and don't come back for a long time.

Q. What is it that you don't like?
A. I don't like all the pink girly stuff. It is too girly. And all those make up games. Too girly.

Q. What makes you laugh?
A. Jokes don't make me laugh out loud. Maybe sometimes. But if someone tickles me I laugh.

Q. How do you like school?
A. I like it but sometimes I don't feel like going. But when I go to school I don't feel like leaving. After I go to school I like it. We talk.

Q. Who are your best friends at school?
A. Mansi, Samaira, Saketh and Harsh.

Q. What do you like about them?
A. Saketh is nice to talk to. But sometimes he says he is thinking about how to help scientists and all. He shakes his fist like this when he does not want to be disturbed. Samaira is very talkative. She can't stop talking. I like Harsh because he is sort of funny. He makes funny faces. Mansi is always talking. Like me.

Q. Did you like Goa?
A. Great. So many beaches. I liked the resort, the sand and the greenery. I'd have liked to stay in a cottage but our room was also nice.

Q. What makes you angry?
A. (Thinks for a long time.) I don't know if I ever get angry. Sometimes when *Amma* shouts.

Q. What are the three things you'll ask God if he were to appear?
A. That I could fly high like a bird.
That I have lots of friends. Every day I have 100 new friends to play with. And more.
That I could do whatever I like to do.

Q. What three things would you like to do first in 'whatever you like to do'?
A. That I could go into the TV and meet all the characters like Mickey Mouse. I'll meet all of them and we can be friends. That I could be an ant and go around the whole house. That I have lots and lots of robots and they could do anything, even read me stories. They can do acrobatics. Tell jokes.

Q. What kind of dreams do you have?
A. In one dream I was doing something. Me, Donald and Goofy were walking in a clubhouse. It was round. We walked out of the clubhouse and I slipped and we slid fast in a cart. Very fast. We fell out of the cart. I had many other dreams – like a scary one once. I was in Mythily attha's house. Nobody was at home. A witch came and said I'll kill you. I said don't kill me now, give me some time. One week. She said she would give me a week and gave me some clay to play with. After one week I was scared again. But I had deep sleep that day so she didn't come because I didn't get any dreams. Only in light sleep you get dreams.

Q. Who told you that?
A. I read in the Children's Encyclopedia.

Q. What do you think of people?
A. Nice. They are very nice. Some are not nice. One day I went to fetch my shuttle cock that fell next door and asked an uncle who was there for it. He made an angry face and said so angrily *'Ellipo. Ledu teesukolevu'* (Go away. You cannot take it.)

Q. Did you get scared?
A. I was scared and ran away. I didn't show him that I was crying. I turned my face away. On the way I started crying and came home.

Q. Are you angry with him?
A. Not much.

Q. What do you like doing alone?
A. Watching TV. Doing art and craft. cards. Writing letters and doing Origami.

Q. You write letters?
A. I wrote to Harsh. And I also wrote to Tinkle.

Q. When did you laugh the most recently?
A. I didn't. I laugh small. But I know once I laughed loudly. It was an ad and the boy's father says pray to God, the mosquitoes will go away. Then the mother lights this card when he is praying. When the boy opens his eyes there are no mosquitoes. Then the father says *Dekha! Macchar nahi kaatenge*. And while he is saying that he leaves the balloon and it goes *phusss*.

Q. Who makes you laugh?
A. Sarvajit. You.

Q. What do you think of yourself?
A. I'm quite funny. And the way I am, I feel quite strange. Sometimes I feel like, who is this Anjali? How did the Earth come to be? Why am I like this? Who made this? Does God really have powers? Is God really there? Is the devil there? Why do they pray? Why do they light *diyas*?

Q. Do you like nature?
A. Yes. If we didn't have plants, there would be no oxygen.

Q. What do you think of adults?
A. Adults are quite strange. Their studies are over. But children have to study. So we have teachers at home and at school – teachers everywhere. I like that adults have no one to tell them anything. Also they don't feel shy.

Q. What are the funny things that adults do?
A. They are different from us. They are very different from us.

Q. Do you feel shy?
A. Sometimes.

Q. Why?
A. *Arre*. I don't know.

Q. You know even adults feel shy don't you?
A. Yeah. But I never see it.

Q. That's because they hide it well.
A. Ummm.

Q. What was your happiest moment?
A. Children's Day every year. Every child will say that.

Q. How can we be happy?
A. By smiling.

Q. That's all?
A. Yes, when I feel happy I smile. When something sad happens I do my favourite things like skipping, watching TV, reading, anything you like. Do it for some time. You start forgetting and enjoy yourself. You start getting happy.

Q. What do you do when people are mean?
A. I tell them they are being mean. Or I tell someone else. Or (laughs) I get angry and don't tell anyone.

Q. What do you think of me?
A. You're funny. You tell me all the stories and do good things… like like being a father.

Q. What about *Mamma*?
A. Good. Though she shouts at me sometimes.

Q. What would do if you were the Prime Minister?
A. I would say don't cut trees or else!

Q. Why don't you want trees to be cut?
A. Because if they cut trees they only won't be there no. So it's better not to cut.

Q. What will you do for children?
A. If I ever see any child working, I will ask who is the owner and tell him not to make the child work. Say no to child labour.

Q. Why?
A. Because children must enjoy life and study.

Q. What is the meaning of life?
A. A place where you have feelings, where you have to do things, something like there's something to do everyday. Not just staying up in heaven.

Q. What do you want to be when you grow up?
A. An archaeologist.

Q. Why?
A. I want to dig and find bones, hidden palaces and new dinosaurs.

Q. What do you think about this world?
A. It's very nice and I do like it. I don't want people to pollute the world. All the people will suffer.

Q. How do you think adults should behave with children?
A. They should be kind. Nice. Many are nice. But some of my friends at school say that their mother or father slapped them. That shouldn't happen. If they make a mistake they will try again, so why must they hit them for no reason. If they hit them nothing will change. You are just making the child have pain for nothing.

They may get good marks or bad marks, it makes no difference. All that will happen is it will hurt. And adults never say sorry also.

Q. How do children feel when adults behave like this?
A. Of course they feel bad.

Q. Do you like giving interviews?
A. A bit. Not so much.

That ended a long interview with the seven-year-old. Thanks Anjali for your time and for your patience. And for your very honest answers.

So we must work and enjoy that process, our happiness is our responsibility, people are by and large nice, life brings something new everyday and adults should be a lot more kinder to their children and to themselves. I agree.

PART 6

HOW TO FLOW WITH ABUNDANCE

93
The Art of Receiving

I watched Anjali receiving a gift from her aunt. First, her eyes opened wide when she saw the gift in her aunt's hand. She asked, with a small nod, "for me?" Then she hopped around her aunt until the gift was handed to her. Once she had the gift in her hands she announced to the rest of us that Nalini *attha* had got her a gift. The gift was then opened with great enthusiasm, and tried out instantly. There were more 'wows' and 'You got it for me?' and other such exclamations. As in most occasions, it ended with a hug for her aunt with a huge, 'thank you.' By now everyone was smiling at the uncorked joy. It happens every single time Anjali receives a gift.

I believe that Anjali's ability to receive with unbounded enthusiasm is one of the many reasons why she gets so many gifts from her indulgent uncles and aunts — toys, dolls, books, chocolates, laddoos, puzzles, clothes and what not. And later, there are endless discussions about how Anjali reacted when she received her gift. Receiving, I realized, is a fine art.

When I gifted copies of my books to a few people, I understood how important it is to receive graciously and enthusiastically. I understood how the giver feels when the recipient shows no grace, no expression. Now, I open gifts as I receive them and share the moment with the giver. I don't view gifts merely as material things. I look at the love behind the gesture.

But one thing is for certain, I can never match the enthusiasm that Anjali brings to receiving.

My way of receiving gifts is to view them with suspicion, wonder what the catch in it is, worry about what I am expected to give in return and sabotage the experience for myself and the giver with this train of thought. Then, wonder why I am not getting any gifts anymore. Can I receive like I deserve to receive it and not as if I got the gift by mistake?

A Return Gift for You: You could get so much more, if you first learn how to receive. Receive all that life brings to you joyfully and enthusiastically and it will bring more. Receive without conditions, without doing anything. Just receive what comes your way gladly, gratefully.

94

A Lesson in Money Consciousness

Anjali got two small pots. She painted one blue and the other black, and then drew some designs on them. After painting, she ran into my study to show me her work. My friend Srinivas Babu who was with me said he would like one, could he take it? She said 'no' and started crying. Babu tried another tactic. Could he buy one?

Anjali liked this idea. She said she would set up her shop in another room and we could buy it from her shop. We visited her 'shop' which was a small table with the two pots on it. I asked her the price. She said that one was ten and another 20, whatever that meant (to her credit she did not say one and two). I gave her a ten-rupee note and bought one. Babu then asked her the price of the other one and she stuck to her price of 20. Babu bought it and got her to paint her name on it. Anjali made a cool 30 bucks just like that!

"I got Rs. 2," she screamed and ran around holding her Rs. 30. I wondered how she got 10 and 20 as her sale price when she had no clue what it meant. I guess, that is the difference between making Rs. 3 and Rs. 30. Good money consciousness.

So how exactly did Anjali's first business deal unfold? First, she added value to two ordinary pots by painting them. Then she put the products in a market place where there were potential buyers with buying power. She priced her products, promoted them, created an interesting atmosphere around the sale, and sold it for a neat profit. Seems you don't need an MBA for that.

My way of creating value is to design a product, keep it to myself, do nothing about it, allow it to die and curse luck. Then, wonder why I never get a break. Does anyone know what I do? Do I know how much to charge? Who am I selling to? And what?

A Return Gift for You: You could make a profitable deal by getting your product catalogue in order with a clear deliverable, price and place. Pitch them to the right market that has the capacity to pay for it and close the deal. Nothing complicated about it.

05 Keep the Flow Going, Every Little Helps

Anjali decided to contribute Rs. 7 to her aunt on her wedding anniversary. This was Anjali's own money of course, saved up over time.

"She told me she has no money," said Anjali as she packed the money into a handmade card she made.

The thought is simple. If someone is in need of something I will contribute my bit. It is not about big or small because every penny helps.

My mother had this quality. She would think of what was necessary in a situation and help quietly, in whatever capacity she could without waiting to be asked. When someone got married, lost a dear one, had a medical issue, excelled at something, was in distress she gave her bit, small or large, but perfectly appropriate. It is a quality I would like to imbibe.

If the philosophers of prosperity are to be believed, it is the attitude of hoarding that stops the energy of money from flowing. Circulate it!

I can give Rs. 7 too. It's better than having grand ideas and giving nothing.

My way of helping someone in trouble is to sense the need, think of helping them, rationalize that I don't have enough for myself and that he would ask if he really needed it anyway. Then, wonder why I don't have great supportive relationships. Can I give what I can without waiting for the other person to ask? Can I understand that it is not how much but how and when I give that's important?

 A Return Gift for You: Be aware of the flow and keep it circulating. What goes around will come around. Surrender to the flow.

96
Don't Think So Much – Buy It

I went to a shoe store with Shobha and Anjali. They bought some footwear. I quietly checked out some shoes for myself and, even more quietly, their prices. After checking a couple, I put the shoes back on the rack. Anjali spotted me, came over and urged – "Buy *Nanna*, what is there to think about? Don't worry about the money. Just buy."

Somehow she sensed my reluctance from across the room and spelt it out for me. I had indeed postponed my decision to buy, worried about spending money. Worried that money would run out. It's a consciousness thing and one that I can deal with only through greater awareness.

My way of generating abundance for myself is to desire lots of things that money can buy, then limit my consciousness with doubt and end up with nothing because I don't want to spend. Then, wonder why I have no money to buy things. Can I trust and spend on myself knowing that my source will not dry up?

 A Return Gift for You: Be aware that we all draw from the same source and strengthen your connection to the source.

A Child's Perspective About Money

This is an excerpt from an interview with Anjali about money.

Q. What do you think of money?
A. You always ask me this question. Money buys things. I played this game called Talking Angela and she said don't worry too much about money because money can't buy you love. It's good to have but it's not everything. You should be happy with what you have.

Q. How much do you want?
A. I don't use any money from my bank account. So, as much as I can collect.

Q. How can we collect money?
A. I keep finding coins. People also give me money sometimes. I also have $2.

Q. How can adults make money?
A. By working.

Q. Do you have to work?
A. Yeah. Even I have to work. If I don't look around I'll never find any money.

This philosophy of Talking Angela is in its own place and Anjali's relationship with money ('as much as I can collect') is in its place. She is quite clear that despite the fact that she doesn't use any money from her account, she does not stop collecting.

But the killer was the final statement. Even she, who merely collects money, has to "look" for money. So stop asking questions like 'do you have to work' and get to work. Reminds me of a conversation I had with an old businessman. His philosophy of business was this – "It's about work and how efficiently you work. Look to enhance your reputation. Money is only a small part of that story. Focus on doing good work and everything else will follow."

My outlook to money is to want it, invite it, put several conditions on it and restrict its flow to me, have no patience to deal with it when it comes and then watch it go away. Then, wonder why money does not enjoy staying with me. Can I be clearer about my relationship with money?

 A Return Gift for You: You could understand that money is a medium of exchange and nothing more. It is not bigger than you. So relax.

Be In The Flow – Money Will Come, Money Will Go

I was trying to engage Anjali.

"Shall we go to the mall?" I asked tentatively.

"Yes!" She jumped. "Yes, yes."

I was apprehensive of her enthusiasm.

"Why are you so happy?" I asked. "So you can buy things there?"

She shrugged her shoulders.

"Yes, we can buy things. Food, toys and other things…"

"Ah, my money will go then," I said, bringing up my main fear.

She shrugged.

"So what? Money will go. Things will come."

So it does. It makes perfect sense.

Money will go. Things will come. Keep the flow going. Don't stop the flow.

Give happily, knowing it will come back.

My approach to spending money is to get uncomfortable with the thought of having money to spend, stress myself over actually spending it and then losing it all double quick in a hurried rush. Then, wonder why the flow of money is erratic. Can I spend comfortably knowing that I get something of value in return?

 A Return Gift for You: You could spend, knowing you have enough to spend.

99
You're Not the Buying Type

Anjali made some startling comments on the prevailing spending behaviours at home.

"You're not the buying kind," she said. "You always think twice before buying and have lots of discussions. And then, you buy less. The only time you bought me something without asking again was when you bought me an extra packet of chips when my friends came home the other day."

What? How do kids notice all of this stuff?

My position of the generous provider now yanked from under my feet, I asked sullenly.

"So who is the buying kind?"

The obvious answer would be the only other adult in the family.

"*Mamma* of course," said Anjali. "She always buys things for me without asking, takes me shopping, tells me what to buy and takes time to buy stuff for me in shops."

I was silent. Truth hurts.

"You also buy *Nanna*," Anjali said, mollifying me a bit. "Just saying that's all."

Okay. Thanks. I will try to spend more heartily.

My way of spending money is to freeze and clam up when the opportunity arrives, send the vibe screaming across the room that I am distressed at the thought of spending and mess up the entire experience for everyone. Then, wonder why nobody's enjoying the experience even after I spent so much money. Can I work on that cautious spending behaviour? Can I be a bit more aware of the thought process in my mind?

A Return Gift for You: You could enhance and enjoy the experience by being wholehearted with your spending – whatever little you decide to spend. Spending money should not be a cause of anxiety; it should be a pleasurable experience. Every spending opportunity is a test for your money consciousness. Enjoy spending.

100
A Thoughtful Anniversary Gift

One expects a card at best, or in most cases, a smile and a hug, on one's wedding anniversary from the children. Most times children don't remember their parent's anniversary which is fine, because the parents barely remember it themselves. It's one of those forgettable dates.

So I was surprised when Anjali asked us both to sit down together as soon as she woke up on our wedding anniversary. We did as told. Then she asked us to close our eyes. When we opened our eyes, we saw a picture of the three of us, mounted on a board with a heart sign enclosing us safely. Then there was her trademark handmade card (with an illustration of a likeness of me on my knees giving flowers to Shobha) and a long note about what we mean to her. It was a beautiful, heartwarming gesture.

But wait. What are these two Rs. 500 notes doing inside the card? At the end of her note to us, she gave us instructions on how to spend the money on ourselves with a gentle hint that we normally do not (spend) on ourselves. Now this was money she saved in her little tin box, gifts from her uncles, aunts, cousins etc on her achievements. I remembered seeing her take the key to the tin box the previous day. She had it all planned.

I told her I will spend, but could she take her money back? She was firm. No. This is my gift for you.

I thanked her. Anjali's anniversary gift financed a fine lunch for Shobha and me. I never imagined eight-year-old kids could think of financing their parents on their anniversaries. I never thought like that. Even now I think twice about spending on my own anniversary. There's much to learn.

My way of buying gifts is to think of a nice gift for someone I love, see the price, reduce budget, think of an alternate gift and mess up the beautiful, original thought. Then, wonder why I don't get beautiful gifts more often. Can I get comfortable with giving and receiving?

A Return Gift for You: Give and receive like a king. You could add that special quality of abundance to transform any experience. It's not how much, but how you do it that matters. Give generously.

www.ingramcontent.com/pod-product-compliance
Lightning Source LLC
Chambersburg PA
CBHW032038150426
43194CB00006B/323